SCIENCE

FOUNDATIONS

Vaccines

Science Foundations: Vaccines

Copyright © 2011 by Infobase Publishing

Chelsea House
An imprint of Infobase Publishing
132 West 31st Street
New York, NY 10001

Library of Congress Cataloging-in-Publication Data
Goldstein, Natalie.
 Vaccines / by Natalie Goldstein.
   p. cm. -- (Science foundations)
 Includes bibliographical references and index.
 ISBN 978-1-60413-339-4 (hardcover)
 1. Vaccines--Popular works. I. Title. II. Series.
 QR189.G65 2010
 615'.372--dc22   2010015733

Chelsea House books are available at special discounts when purchased in bulk quantities for businesses, associations, institutions, or sales promotions. Please call our Special Sales Department in New York at (212) 967-8800 or (800) 322-8755.

You can find Chelsea House on the World Wide Web at
http://www.chelseahouse.com

Text design by Kerry Casey
Cover design by Alicia Post
Composition by EJB Publishing Services
Cover printed by Bang Printing, Brainerd, MN
Book printed and bound by Bang Printing, Brainerd, MN
Date printed: December 2010
Printed in the United States of America

10 9 8 7 6 5 4 3 2 1

This book is printed on acid-free paper.

All links and Web addresses were checked and verified to be correct at the time of publication. Because of the dynamic nature of the Web, some addresses and links may have changed since publication and may no longer be valid.

Contents

Ancients and Aristocrats

In the autumn of 1717, Lady Mary Wortley Montagu attended a party like none she had ever been to before. Lady Montagu was a true blue blood—a wealthy British aristocrat who had been to countless balls and parties held at the mansions of her privileged friends and even in the palace of the king and queen of England. Yet none of these festivities prepared her for her experience at the party that she attended in Constantinople (Turkey), modern Istanbul, that fall.

Mary had accompanied her aristocratic husband, Lord Montagu, to his new post as the British ambassador to Turkey. Unlike other diplomatic wives, Lady Montagu did not spend her days at the embassy giving tea parties for other British ladies. No, Mary Montagu was a spirited and fiercely independent woman. She alone among all the other diplomats' wives dared to dress in the Turkish fashion and even went out unaccompanied to explore the exotic Turkish city on her own. During her explorations of Constantinople she met many Turks. Through her new acquaintances, she learned about and was invited to an unusual party.

Only three years earlier, Lady Montagu had fallen ill with a terrible and deadly disease—**smallpox**. She was lucky to have survived. Her brother had died from the disease. She was determined that her children would not contract smallpox, but in eighteenth-century Europe no one knew how to prevent it or cure it. What Lady

Figure 1.1 British aristocrat Lady Mary Wortley Montagu, seen here in Turkish clothing circa 1720, had her children inoculated against smallpox in Turkey, and then touted the vaccine back home in London.

Montagu learned on her wanderings through Constantinople was that the Turks had found a way to prevent people from contracting smallpox. The procedure was so common and considered so safe that the Turks actually performed it at parties where one could be saved from smallpox while eating fine food and having a good time. In a letter, Lady Montagu stated, "People send to one another to know if any of their family has a mind to have the smallpox: they make up parties for this purpose."

Lady Montagu was escorted to the party by a Turkish friend. The party was held at the home of a local resident. There were about 15 other people at the party. They were eating and enjoying themselves when an old woman came into the house to begin the "medical" part of the party. Lady Montagu wrote in the same letter: "There is a set of old women who make it their business to perform the operation every autumn, in the month of September, when the great heat is abated [lessened]." Because this was her first "smallpox party," Lady Montagu simply watched the procedure as it was carried out. In letters to friends, Mary described how the old woman set out a nutshell that contained some **pus** from the sores of a person who had contracted smallpox. One by one, the partygoers sat next to the old woman. She asked each person kindly which arm they wanted her to cut. Each person stretched out an arm, and the old woman made a small cut in a vein. Then she carefully dipped a needle into the pus-filled nutshell and inserted the needle into the vein.

In her letters, Lady Montagu used the term *engrafting* to describe this procedure. Of course, she was interested not only in how the procedure was carried out but also in whether it harmed the person who was infected with the smallpox pus. Mary arranged to meet with some of the people who had been at the party she'd attended. Over the next few weeks, she met with and talked to several of them to determine the effects that engrafting had on them. She reported what she discovered in letters to her friends back in England, noting that the people were healthy and felt fine for the first few days after the engrafting. Lady Montagu further reported, "Then the fever begins to seize them, and they keep to their beds for two days, very seldom three." At the end of two or three days of a slight fever, all the people were once again fine. More important, none of them ever contracted smallpox. "There is no example of anyone that has died of it [engrafting]," she wrote, "and you may believe I am very well satisfied of the safety of this experiment, since I intend to try it on my dear little son."

Lady Montagu convinced Lord Montagu of the safety of engrafting. Having persuaded her husband to allow her to have their young son engrafted with smallpox, she took her son to an engrafting party, and he bravely underwent the procedure. After a couple of days of fever, he was fine. Though smallpox **epidemics**—widespread outbreaks of a disease that affect many people—raged on and off for years, Lady Montagu's son never got the disease. Engrafting had protected him and made his body **immune** to—or able to fight off—smallpox.

ANCIENT INOCULATIONS

Engrafting was Lady Montagu's word for what today is called **inoculation**. Inoculation is the introduction of an infectious substance into the body to build the body's immunity against the disease it causes. Although ancient people had no notion of immunity or of how the body's immune system worked, many different cultures had developed different forms of inoculation to prevent disease.

China

More than 1,000 years ago, Chinese healers observed that, for some reason they could not understand, people who had suffered from smallpox and survived never got the disease again. Epidemics of smallpox had been ravaging China for centuries, so healers had many opportunities to observe the characteristics of the disease. They knew that this terrible illness began with a high fever and severe headache. These symptoms were soon followed by the eruption of extremely painful, burning sores all over the body, including in the mouth and the throat. Most sufferers experienced painful body spasms. In its worst, most deadly form, smallpox causes bleeding inside the body. Sometimes victims also bleed from the nose and the eyes. Everyone who got this **hemorrhagic** form of smallpox was doomed. Even in its non-bleeding form, smallpox was almost always fatal.

Needless to say, people were terrified of getting smallpox. Chinese healers who studied the disease made an important observation. They noticed that even people who got a very mild form of the illness never got smallpox again. They concluded, correctly, that there was something about being exposed to smallpox that prevented the disease from returning. They did not know why the person was protected or what protected him, but they acted on this observation to develop one of the earliest forms of inoculation. Smallpox was such a horrific disease that Chinese doctors decided that it was worth the risk to deliberately infect people with smallpox to help them become immune to the disease.

The ancient Chinese healers treated mainly children who had had no exposure to the illness. In preparing the inoculation, Chinese doctors began by collecting the scabs that had formed over the sores on the bodies of sufferers who had contracted only a mild form of smallpox. They ground up the scabs to form a powder. The powder was then placed in thin tubes made of ivory. An ivory tube was placed into a child's nose, and the child was told to inhale the powder. The effects were the same as those observed by Lady Montagu in Turkey. After a few days, the children developed a fever. Some got a few, tiny smallpox sores. After a few days, the fever and the sores disappeared. Most of these inoculated children never got smallpox.

Africa

Highly observant healers were not limited to ancient China. Ancient African civilizations also knew about inoculation against smallpox. In many parts of the continent, healers had people eat the scabs taken

Inoculation in Ancient India

Ancient texts from India reveal that thousands of years ago, Buddhist monks used a type of inoculation to help them develop a resistance to snake venom. The inoculation process took some time. At first, the monk would swallow a very tiny amount of the venom from a highly poisonous and deadly snake such as the king cobra. A while later, the monk would take another dose of snake venom. Over time, the dose of snake venom was increased. At some point, the monks determined that they had taken enough of the snake venom to make their bodies immune to its effects. Thus, if a monk was bitten by a poisonous snake, he would not die from the snake bite because his body had developed a type of immunity to the snake venom.

from others who had had a mild case of smallpox. In other parts of Africa, healers scratched a person's skin just enough to reveal blood. Into the small wound the healer put some fluid taken from the sores of a person who had a mild form of smallpox. Both of these methods worked to develop immunity in the inoculated people, most of whom never contracted smallpox.

Of course, in the ancient world, healers had no idea why these methods worked. They did not know anything about the immune system or the development of resistance to disease. Also, their methods were inexact. Occasionally, healers' inoculations were made out of a strong and dangerous strain of the disease. In these cases, the inoculated person might get a severe case of smallpox and die. Sometimes healers used too much or too little inoculant, so the recipient either got sick or did not develop immunity.

Wary Westerners

Four years after Lady Montagu's son had been inoculated against smallpox, the Montagu family was called back to England. In 1721, a smallpox epidemic broke out in London. Lady Montagu realized with horror that her daughter had not yet been inoculated against the disease. She met with the most respected doctors in London and tried to persuade them of the safety of the smallpox inoculation. It took a lot of persuasion before one doctor finally agreed to inoculate Mary's daughter. A group of doctors, certain that the procedure would kill the patient, kept a close watch on the girl. After a few days of fever, she was fine. The medical men continued to keep tabs on the Montagu children while they did the best they could to treat the thousands of smallpox cases in the city. Just as Lady Montagu had predicted, neither of her children came down with smallpox.

Princess Caroline, who was married to the future king of England (George II), was Mary Montagu's friend. The princess was concerned for her children and considered having them inoculated. She saw how effective inoculation had been in Mary's children, but she was a far more cautious woman than Mary. In an experiment that foreshadows shameful things to come, Princess Caroline insisted that poor orphans be given smallpox inoculations first. If they survived, then she would have her more worthy, "royal" children inoculated. All the inoculated orphans survived. (Had they not survived,

Figure 1.2 This carved wooden statue of Shapona, the West African god of smallpox, is adorned with layers of meaningful objects such as monkey skulls, cowrie shells, and nails. Smallpox was thought to be a disease foisted upon humans due to Shapona's "divine displeasure," and formal worship of the god of smallpox was highly controlled by specific priests in charge of shrines to the god.

she figured, who would have cared?) Thus, Princess Caroline had her children inoculated against smallpox, and all survived the procedure. Though the princess's concerns are understandable, her insistence that more "lowly" and "expendable" people be tested first became a shameful practice that was to arise in coming centuries as inoculations for other diseases were developed.

It was not until medical science became quite advanced that doctors understood why and how inoculation worked; however, that understanding would take more than a century. Doctors in the Western world, including Europe and the United States, were wary of inoculation against smallpox, thinking it too risky. It took a long time before Western medicine would adopt and refine this ancient method of preventing disease.

Edward Jenner and the Milkmaid

It was the most terrifying experience of his life—one he would never forget. In 1757, when Edward Jenner was only eight years old, his older brother with whom he was living (Edward, the eighth of nine children, was orphaned when he was five years old) sent him to a nearby English village to be inoculated against smallpox. A smallpox epidemic was raging in that part of England, and his brother wanted to protect Edward against the disease. Yet the process of inoculation in England at that time was nothing like the "parties" Lady Montagu had attended in Turkey. The process of inoculation in eighteenth-century England was more like torture than a pleasant get-together.

Before he was inoculated, Edward suffered through a period of starvation when he was given almost no food. While hunger gnawed at him, he was bled several times. Bleeding was a common practice then because doctors at that time believed that impure "humors" lived in the blood. Only by bleeding could the bad blood be gotten out of the body. Bleeding entailed cutting into a vein, usually in the arm, and allowing quantities of blood to drip into a bowl. By ridding the body of the "bad" blood the doctors thought they were getting rid of its impurities. As an adult, Edward Jenner later described his experience: "There was bleeding till the blood was thin; purging [weight loss] till the body was wasted to a skeleton; and starving . . .

to keep it so." Doctors prescribed this ordeal because they believed—incredibly—that starvation and bleeding made the body stronger. Of course, now we know it does just the opposite.

After suffering through many days of this torment, young Edward was locked inside a barn. There he saw a group of starved and terrified boys just like him, who were waiting to be inoculated. Another group of boys in the barn had been inoculated a week or two previously. They lay on the dirty straw, tossing and shaking with fever, many having broken out in smallpox sores. Edward stared at them in sheer terror. A doctor entered the barn, took out a knife, leaned down beside a sick boy, and cut off part of a smallpox sore. Then he beckoned to a boy in Edward's group. The doctor used the knife to make a cut in the boy's arm and to push the material from the smallpox sore into the wound.

After being inoculated in this way, Edward and the boys in his group were kept in the barn for several more weeks. Edward and the other boys continued to be starved; they got weaker and weaker. Worse than the hunger was their fear of the smallpox fever that was to come. Sure enough, after about two weeks, Edward and every other boy in his group came down with a high fever. Soon after, the painful, open smallpox sores erupted on their skin. The fever and sores lasted another week or two. Only when the sores had dried up and fallen off were Edward and the boys allowed—finally—to leave the barn. Edward returned home. He was famished and shaken, but he was also now immune to smallpox. This experience had so traumatized young Edward Jenner that he determined to find a way to inoculate people against smallpox without putting them through such a terrible ordeal.

When Edward Jenner grew up, he became a doctor. He was determined to find a way to prevent smallpox and, if possible, to cure it. Jenner practiced medicine in the rural countryside of Gloucestershire, England, his patients being mainly farmers and the simple folk who worked for them. Jenner treated his patients for common illnesses and broken bones and such, but he was ever on the lookout for information about smallpox. In caring for his rural patients, Jenner had heard them describe how farm workers who tended cows and had contracted cowpox never got smallpox. Most rural doctors thought this idea was pure superstition, a crazy notion perpetuated by ignorant country folk. Jenner was not so sure. He had heard this

Figure 2.1 Edward Jenner, the doctor who is credited with discovering the first vaccine to prevent smallpox, is shown vaccinating James Phipps, on May 14, 1796. He used pus from the hand of infected dairy maid Sarah Nelmes.

belief repeated so many times by so many farmers that he began to wonder if there was some truth to it.

For several years, Jenner kept a notebook in which he recorded everything he could find out about people who had contracted cowpox. He studied the way the disease was passed from cows to humans and the course of the disease in infected farm workers. For example, in 1778, Jenner visited a farmer who had contracted cowpox. The farmer, William Smith, told Jenner that he had gotten cowpox after milking one of his cows that had the disease. Jenner examined the farmer's hands, which contained cowpox sores. Then he examined the cow. He saw that the cow had cowpox sores all over its udders. Obviously, what the farmer said was likely true; he had gotten cowpox when some material from the cow's sores entered a small cut in the skin on his hands.

Farmer Smith's experience reminded Jenner of his inoculation, when the disease material was introduced into his body through a cut made in his arm. His conversation with the farmer also revealed that cowpox in humans was almost identical to a mild case of small-pox. Both cowpox and mild smallpox made the people who got one or the other immune to the more deadly form of smallpox. Perhaps, Jenner thought, cowpox and smallpox are related. Could they be different forms of the same disease? If they were related, could cowpox be used to inoculate people against smallpox?

Jenner was determined to find out. Jenner later (1793) wrote, "During the investigation of [naturally acquired] cowpox, I was struck by the idea that it might be practical to [breed] the disease by inoculation, after the manner of smallpox; first from the cow, and finally from one human being to another." To test his idea, Jenner had to undertake a highly risky experiment.

THE MILKMAID

To test his theory, Jenner first had to locate someone who had cowpox. In 1796, he was introduced to a young milkmaid named Sarah Nelmes. Sarah had recently acquired cowpox, and she had a few cowpox sores on her hands from milking an infected cow. Jenner asked Sarah if she would take part in his experiment, and she agreed.

Now Jenner had to find a healthy person who he could inoculate with Sarah's cowpox. Finding someone who was willing to be deliberately infected with a disease was a lot harder than finding Sarah.

After asking around among his patients, Jenner finally found eight-year-old James Phipps. Phipps's father agreed to the experiment because he wanted to protect his son from getting the deadlier form of smallpox. Jenner described his experiment in these words: "The more accurately to observe the progress of the infection I selected a healthy boy, about eight years old, for the purpose of inoculating for cowpox. The cowpox matter was taken from a sore on the hand of a dairymaid, who was infected by her master's cows, and it was inserted on the arm of the boy by means of two superficial incisions [shallow cuts] . . . each about an inch [2.5 centimeters] long."

After the inoculation, Jenner carefully observed the boy every day. Seven days after getting the cowpox inoculation, James Phipps developed a case of cowpox. Phipps was mildly ill for only one day. After 24 hours, his headache, fever, and chills completely disappeared. The boy was once again completely healthy. Now came the really dangerous part of the experiment.

The First Credit for the Smallpox Vaccine

Unknown to Edward Jenner, or to anyone else, an obscure English farmer had successfully done in 1774 what Jenner famously did decades later. In that year, cattle breeder Benjamin Jesty decided to test the popular superstition about cowpox preventing smallpox. Jesty inoculated members of his family with some material taken from cowpox sores on one of his infected cattle. Each member of his family had a few days of mild symptoms, and then each was fine. When smallpox broke out after that, no one in the Jesty family ever got the disease. For some reason, Jesty never told anyone about what he had done and how successful it had been in preventing smallpox. For that reason, Edward Jenner—not Jesty—is credited with discovering how to use cowpox to vaccinate against smallpox.

THE ULTIMATE TEST

Jenner had to find out if inoculation with cowpox made young James Phipps immune to smallpox. The only way to do that was to deliberately infect him with deadly smallpox. Jenner knew how risky this was. If his theory was correct, the boy would not develop small-pox. Yet if Jenner's idea was wrong, the boy might die of the disease. Still, Jenner had no choice.

In his notes, Jenner wrote, "On the 1st of July [the boy] was inoc-ulated with [smallpox pus] immediately taken from a pustule [open sore]. Several slight punctures and incisions were made in both his arms and the matter was carefully inserted." Jenner waited nervous-ly to see what would happen. He visited Phipps every day for several weeks. The boy showed no signs of coming down with smallpox. Jen-ner was delighted; his inoculation with cowpox had made Phipps im-mune to the deadly human smallpox. Jenner later described "the joy I felt at the prospect before me of being the instrument destined to take away from the world one of its greatest calamities." Edward Jen-ner published the results of his experiment in a four-page pamphlet. In this pamphlet, Jenner coined the word *vaccine*, which comes from the Latin for cow (*vacca*). From that time on, the term *vaccine* was used to refer to any substance that triggers an immune response that protects against a disease without actually causing the disease. Soon, the term *vaccination* was used to describe inoculation. In his pamphlet, Jenner explained that "What renders the cowpox virus so extremely singular is that the person who has been thus affected is forever after secure from the infection of the smallpox."

Jenner's slim pamphlet became an instant sensation throughout the medical community in England. Some doctors thought Jenner was brilliant and wanted to try his form of inoculation immediately on their own patients. Other doctors thought Jenner's ideas danger-ous and loudly opposed them. Many were outraged that a trained doctor would "waste" his time trying to prove the truth of igno-rant farmers' superstitions. They called his experimental success a "lucky accident." Arguments for and against vaccination raged across Britain.

More scientifically minded doctors took the risk of repeating Jenner's experiment. All of them got the same results. One London physician who performed Jenner's experiment wrote a letter to Jenner stating, "I think substituting the cowpox poison for the smallpox promises to be one of the greatest improvements that has ever been made in medicine." Over time, Jenner's vaccination procedure became the accepted way to prevent smallpox.

Neither Jenner, nor any other doctors of his time, knew why vaccination worked. They did not know about the body's immune system. They did not know that germs cause disease. For these reasons, there were several drawbacks to Jenner's vaccination. First, the vaccine was made from live viruses taken from cowpox sores. Unbeknownst to Jenner, the cowpox material had to be "active," or taken from the cow at just the right time, for the vaccine to be effective. Second, the active cowpox material did not stay active for long once it was outside the cow's body. Therefore, distributing viable vaccine was another problem. Finally, though Jenner claimed that

Outrage and Opposition

Some doctors and other professionals—especially clergymen—opposed Jenner's ideas on religious grounds. Not only did they believe that diseases were punishments that came from God, but they also were outraged that a disease of cows could be related to a disease of humans. This offended their understanding of humanity's place as above and superior to "lower" animals. Jenner's work was, therefore, ungodly and even blasphemous.

One incensed critic wrote, "Smallpox is a visitation from God and originates in man, but the cowpox is produced by presumptuous, impious men. The former [smallpox] Heaven ordained [ordered], the latter [cowpox] is perhaps a daring and profane [sinful] violation of our holy order."

The notion that disease is a divine punishment goes back hundreds, even thousands, of years. It was a concept that helped people throughout the world, in many civilizations, to understand as best they could why terrible diseases such as smallpox afflicted humankind.

his vaccination protected a person against smallpox forever, in fact, immunity to smallpox lasted only about seven years. (Even today's smallpox vaccine does not provide lifelong protection.) Despite these shortcomings, Jenner's groundbreaking work would prove to be the first step medical science took in its understanding of germs and of what would much later become the field of immunology, or the study of the immune system. Jenner will always be remembered as the first doctor who proved the effectiveness of vaccines.

Discovering What Works

As a child, Louis Pasteur was very ordinary. There was nothing about him that indicated that he would grow up to be one of the most brilliant and celebrated medical researchers of all time.

Pasteur grew up in a small town in France. Though he was a so-so student, he did manage to earn a place in a college in Paris, where he studied chemistry. By all accounts, Pasteur's college career was also unremarkable. He got married as soon as he graduated and began looking for a job. He was hired as a professor of science by a college in the city of Lille. There Pasteur remained for several years, earning a reputation as a fine scientist and teacher.

Pasteur first gained national renown when, in 1856, Emperor Napoleon III asked him to figure out what was destroying the fine French wines the nation was famous for. After conducting several brilliant experiments and spending long hours peering into his **microscope**, Pasteur discovered that the wine was being ruined by a type of **microbe**. The microbe was contaminating the wine and spoiling it. Pasteur had all the winemakers destroy their microbe-infested wine. Then he showed them how to heat their wine to kill any unwanted microbes that might be contaminating it. Pasteur had saved the French wine industry. He was hailed as a national hero.

Several years after this success, Pasteur was again called upon to save another important French industry. A strange disease was

Figure 3.1 French chemist and microbiologist Louis Pasteur was the first to prove that bacteria spread diseases.

killing the silkworms that French clothmakers used to make silk. Throughout France the silkworms were dying. The silk makers were desperate. Again, Pasteur saved the day. After five years of intensive research, Pasteur identified the microbe that was killing the silkworms. The disease-causing agent was a **parasite** that was passed from silkworm to silkworm via their droppings. Silkworms feed on mulberry tree leaves. Droppings left by an infected silkworm on the mulberry leaves passed the microbe on to the other silkworms that also fed on these leaves. Again, Pasteur had the silk makers destroy all of their infected mulberry trees and all of their silkworms and start afresh with newborn, uninfected silkworms that could feed on new, uninfected trees. Though starting over from scratch cost the silkmakers a lot of money, they were grateful that Pasteur had found the cause of the disease. Now they, too, could use a microscope to look at mulberry leaves to make sure they contained no disease-causing parasites. Pasteur had done it again. He had saved another French industry.

As the news of this triumph spread, Pasteur became the most famous and honored man in all of France.

GERMS AND DISEASE

Pasteur was one of the great scientists who demonstrated the truth of **germ theory**. Germ theory states that each particular disease is caused by one particular microbe, or tiny disease-causing agent. Before germ theory was proved, doctors really had no idea what caused disease. Yet once Pasteur and other scientists showed that one germ causes one specific disease, medical researchers could begin looking for ways to kill particular disease-causing germs.

The germ theory of disease arose from key scientific discoveries. For example, in the late 1600s, Dutchman Anton van Leeuwenhoek (*LAY vuhn huk*) first discovered the existence of microbes. Though he earned his living running a dry goods store, van Leeuwenhoek was obsessed with making lenses (a new technology at the time). He spent all of his spare time perfecting his lenses. Eventually, he used one of his best lenses to build the world's first microscope. Peering into his microscope at a droplet of rain, for example, van Leeuwenhoek was astonished to see an entire universe of tiny, moving things. These were microbes, which van Leeuwenhoek first called "animalcules" (little animals) and sometimes "little beasties." Van Leeuwenhoek was correct in observing that microbes, invisible to the unaided eye, had all the characteristics of animals. Van Leeuwenhoek had discovered an entire world of living things no one had ever seen before.

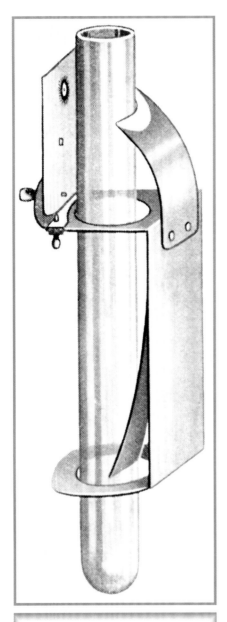

Figure 3.2 A historical engraving shows an early microscope created by Anton van Leeuwenhoek. His microscopes used a single lens (mounted here as a flat sheet in the upper left), which he ground to near-perfection himself. A test tube rests in the middle.

After many decades of debate, van Leeuwenhoek's discovery of microbes and his invention of the microscope enabled scientists to prove the germ theory of disease. Though scientists, such as Pasteur, were staunch supporters of the germ theory of disease, they could not always identify the microbe that caused a particular disease. Some microbes, like the relatively large **bacteria**, were easy to see under a microscope. Yet disease-causing agents that no microscope could reveal still seemed to exist. (Later, scientists would learn that these diseases were caused by **viruses**.) Still, the "one germ, one illness" theory allowed scientists to discover ways to treat all types of disease, whether caused by bacteria, viruses, or other **pathogens**. Louis Pasteur was a pioneer in the development of early vaccines to fight disease.

SAVING SHEEP

Anthrax is a dreadful disease that mostly affects sheep and other farm animals, though it can infect and kill people as well. No one knew what caused it or how to fight it. This mystery intrigued Pasteur, and he decided that he was going to conquer anthrax.

In 1881, Pasteur packed up his microscope and other lab equipment and moved to a rural area of France, where hundreds of sheep were dying of anthrax. Pasteur examined the blood and other tissues of infected sheep. It did not take him long to identify the bacteria that caused anthrax. The real problem was figuring out how to fight it. Pasteur worked for months trying to make a vaccine that would confer immunity against anthrax. The first thing he had to do was weaken, or **attenuate**, the anthrax bacteria. Pasteur had made a key discovery earlier when he, quite by accident, learned how to make

Spontaneous Generation

Before scientists like Pasteur and others finally proved that germ theory was true, most scientists and doctors believed in **spontaneous generation**. Spontaneous generation was the concept that life could spring spontaneously from matter such as decaying meat. The notion was supported by observations that meat that was left out for a while seemed suddenly to produce maggots and flies, which crawled all over it. After the discovery of the microscope, broth, too, seemed to spontaneously generate countless microbes, which swarmed in it. Where could these critters come from except from the meat or broth itself?

Some scientists resisted the idea that flies could come from meat. They tried to prove that flies, like all other living things, came from other (parent) flies. It took a long time (hundreds of years) and the tireless work of many scientists, but eventually the notion of spontaneous generation was proved false. It was, in fact, Louis Pasteur who put the final nail in the coffin of spontaneous generation. Pasteur put sterilized (microbe-free) broth in specially shaped flasks that he hoped would keep microbes out. The flasks allowed air to enter but not dust. After several days, Pasteur examined the broth. It still contained no microbes. Pasteur's experiment showed that the broth did not "create" microbes. The microbes entered the sterilized broth only by being carried into it on dust motes in the air. Spontaneous generation was dead.

the microbes used in a vaccine sufficiently weak so that they would not cause disease in the animal or person being vaccinated.

Two years earlier, Pasteur had been doing research on a deadly chicken disease called chicken cholera. Pasteur had worked so hard he became totally exhausted. His wife insisted that he take two weeks off and go on vacation. So, in the summer of 1879, Pasteur and his family left for a couple of weeks of relaxation. Before he left his lab, Pasteur asked his lab assistants to keep the chicken cholera germs alive while he was gone. He instructed his assistants to transfer the germs that were growing in old chicken broth into freshly made chicken broth every couple of days. The newly made chicken broth would keep the cholera microbes alive.

Alas, Pasteur's assistants were not as reliable or trustworthy as they should have been. Instead of doing what Pasteur had asked them to do, the assistants decided that they, too, needed a vacation. Off they went, leaving the germs in the same old broth for two weeks. When Pasteur got back, he was furious. But, lacking any other source of chicken cholera germs, he injected some of the old broth into a few healthy chickens. Pasteur and his shamefaced assistants expected the chickens to die. They were amazed when the chickens remained healthy. Pasteur reprimanded his assistants, correctly claiming that the chickens did not die because the germs in the old broth had gotten too weak. The lab assistants brewed up a new batch of broth in which they grew new, more vigorous chicken cholera germs. Pasteur then injected these dangerous, living germs into the chickens. Pasteur thought that now, surely, the chickens would die from cholera. Pasteur was astounded when none of the chickens died, or even got sick. He then realized that the weakened germs they had previously been given had made them immune to the active and deadly form of the germ. Pasteur had made a key breakthrough in the development of vaccines. He had learned how to weaken, or attenuate, disease microbes so they could be safely used in a vaccine.

Anthrax was such a lethal disease that Pasteur knew he had to attenuate his vaccine quite a lot before it would be safe. The anthrax bacteria had to be made so weak they would not cause anthrax when used in a vaccine. Pasteur spent months attenuating his vaccine until he felt it was safe to use. When he announced to the public that he had created a vaccine that could prevent anthrax, people were skeptical. A very annoyed Pasteur decided to do his vaccination experiments in public to prove the skeptics wrong.

On May 5, 1881, Pasteur visited a nearby farm. A crowd had gathered to watch him work. Pasteur divided the farmer's animals into two equal groups, with each group having 24 sheep, a goat, and 6 cows. One group was inoculated with a highly attenuated anthrax vaccine. He left the second group of animals unvaccinated. The inoculated animals did not become ill. Two weeks later, in view of another crowd of onlookers, Pasteur inoculated the first group of animals with a stronger, though still attenuated, vaccine. Again, after several weeks none of the inoculated animals came down with anthrax.

On May 31, Pasteur did the final—and most important—part of his experiment. In front of a huge crowd, he injected all the animals in both groups with an unattenuated deadly strain of live anthrax bacteria. Within two days, all the unfortunate animals in the uninoculated group died of anthrax. All the animals that had been inoculated with the vaccine remained perfectly healthy. Once again, this brilliant man had made a scientific breakthrough. He showed that an attenuated vaccine could be made that was effective in preventing anthrax.

MAD DOGS

As a young boy, Pasteur had seen one of his friends die a horrific death after being bitten by a rabid wolf. Rabies is a terrible disease that affects the brain and other parts of the nervous system, causing convulsions and making it impossible for a person to swallow. Pasteur's young friend had received the only treatment known at that time. A red-hot iron was plunged into the boy's wound in the hope that the fiery heat would kill the infection. In this case, as in most others, the treatment did not work, and the boy died choking and convulsing. Among animals, the brain infection and the inability to swallow torment them and drive them "mad." In this condition they may bite any living thing they come across. The disease is then passed on through the germs in their saliva to the person or animal that they bite.

Pasteur decided to take on the challenge of finding a vaccine to prevent rabies. This was the toughest goal he had ever set himself. His problems began right away, as he searched—in vain—for the microbe that causes rabies. No matter what type of tissue he examined, his microscope showed no signs of a germ that causes rabies. Pasteur concluded that rabies must be caused by a germ that is "invisible." (We now know that rabies is caused by a virus.) He determined that this problem would not stop him. He would continue to seek a vaccine in the same way he had done before, as if he were working with a visible microbe.

Now You See It, Now You Don't: Anthrax Unmasked

For ages, people had wondered why anthrax would strike suddenly and then disappear, only to strike again much later. What caused this on-again, off-again behavior?

Another brilliant physician and pioneer in germ theory, Robert Koch, also studied anthrax. Not only did he grow anthrax in his lab, but he eventually was able to determine the microbe's life cycle. Koch found that anthrax existed in two forms: as microbes, called **bacilli**, and as **spores** (a type of "seed"). Koch discovered that farm animals contracted anthrax when they ate grass that contained anthrax spores. When lying around on grass or in soil, the spores are not active. Yet when an animal ingests the spores, they change their form. Inside the animal's body the spores change into microbes. The microbes reproduce rapidly inside the animal's body. They infect many of its tissues and, within a couple of days, the animal dies. Yet before the animal dies, the bacilli change back into spores. The spores are deposited on the soil and grass when the animal's dead body begins to decay. There the spores will wait—surviving heat and cold, rain and drought—until another animal comes along and gobbles them up.

Pasteur knew that rabies was a disease of the nervous system. After four years of intense research, he was able to create an attenuated vaccine made out of the ground-up spinal cords of rabid rabbits. He began by deliberately infecting luckless rabbits with rabies. Then he used tissue taken from the spinal cords of these rabbits to infect other rabbits with rabies. From these experiments, Pasteur learned that the germs were present in the spinal cord. What took him four years to figure out was how to attenuate these microbes. He discovered that allowing the spinal cords of infected rabbits to dry out for 14 days greatly weakened the germ

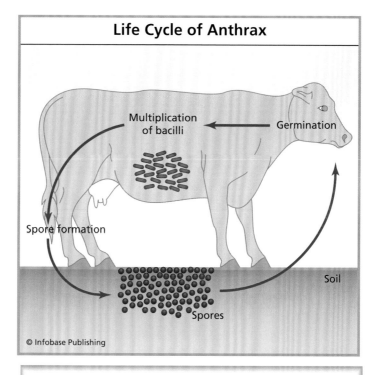

Figure 3.3   This illustration shows the life cycle of anthrax. This bacillus can form dormant spores that are able to survive long periods of time in harsh conditions. When the spores are ingested, inhaled, or come into contact with an open wound on a host, they reactivate and quickly multiply.

that caused rabies. Pasteur was ready to test his attenuated rabies vaccine.

Pasteur began by injecting a few dogs with a very much weakened form of the vaccine. After a few weeks, the dogs showed no signs of the disease. Over the next month or so, every couple of weeks Pasteur inoculated the dogs with ever-stronger doses of attenuated rabies vaccine. Still, the dogs remained healthy. Then came the supreme test. Each of the vaccinated dogs was given an injection of live, deadly rabies germs. None of the dogs became ill. Pasteur had triumphed again. All the dogs had developed an immunity to rabies from Pasteur's attenuated vaccine.

Now, Pasteur faced the riskiest, most daunting part of his experiment. He had to test his vaccine on humans. Yet what person would willingly be injected with a vaccine that might end up giving him or her a disease as dreadful as rabies? Finding a volunteer for this part of the experiment took time. In July 1885, Pasteur was told about a nine-year-old boy who had been bitten by a rabid dog. The boy's mother took him to Pasteur's lab in Paris. Both of them were desperate and willing to take a chance on the vaccine. After all, even if the vaccine did not work, the boy would die of rabies anyway. The boy had nothing to lose, so he agreed to be vaccinated.

In the course of the next 10 days, the boy received injections of the rabies vaccine. The first injections contained the most attenuated vaccine. Each day, the strength of the vaccine was increased. By the tenth day, the boy was dosed with fairly potent rabies germs. After the 10-day treatment was complete, Pasteur and the boy waited. Pasteur was very anxious, and he examined the boy every day for signs of rabies. Day after day, no signs of the disease were found. After several weeks, the boy was still healthy. Pasteur was ecstatic. He had saved the boy's life and discovered a vaccine that could prevent this terrible disease.

Inspired by Pasteur's groundbreaking work, scientists began searching for vaccines to combat other dreaded diseases. Following in the great Frenchman's footsteps, many biologists attempted to create attenuated vaccines to fight disease. They found that attenuated vaccines did not always work, or were sometimes too dangerous to administer (because they sometimes caused the disease), so another approach had to be found.

Pasteur had experimented with "killed" vaccines. These are vaccines that have had their active, infectious components killed, or rendered inactive, by a chemical. Pasteur often used **formalin**, a chemical related to formaldehyde, to kill the active parts of a disease-causing microbe, or pathogen. For reasons he did not understand, in some cases inoculation with these "dead" pathogens caused the body to develop immunity to the disease.

In the 1880s, other biologists began experimenting with "killed" microbe vaccines. Teams of researchers used chemicals to kill the pathogen that causes swine fever (hog cholera), and their vaccine worked well in preventing this disease among inoculated pigs. Other scientists found methods of killing microbes by applying heat or bombarding them with radiation. Some of these techniques led to the creation of effective vaccines to prevent tuberculosis, cholera, and bubonic plague.

ANTITOXINS

Medical researchers were working feverishly to develop new vaccines to prevent all sorts of diseases. One disease that biologists were intent on defeating was diphtheria, a dreadful affliction that mainly affects children and that often causes death by suffocation. In diphtheria, a false membrane (pseudomembrane) forms on affected tissues in the throat, the nose, and the respiratory system. As the disease progresses, it attacks the central nervous system and may cause paralysis. At a research institute in Berlin, Germany, in the late 1880s, scientists Emil von Behring and Shibasaburo Kitasato were determined to destroy diphtheria once and for all. (Similar work on diphtheria was being done simultaneously by Émile Roux and Alexandre Yersin at the Pasteur Institute in Paris.) Behring discovered that it was not the diphtheria bacteria (*Corynebacterium diphtheria*) itself that harms and kills the body. It was a deadly substance—a **toxin** (poison)—produced by the bacteria that did the damage. Because the main agent is a poison and not a microbe, ordinary vaccines that killed microbes were ineffective against diphtheria. Von Behring would have to find another way to attack diphtheria.

Behring analyzed the toxin produced by *C. diphtheria*. He then injected a tiny amount of the toxin into guinea pigs. The animals did

Figure 3.4 In 1901, German physiologist Emil von Behring won the first ever Nobel Prize in Medicine.

not become ill. When Behring examined their blood, he saw that it contained a substance that might be able to fight the toxin. He carefully separated this substance, which he called an **antitoxin**, and blood serum (the clear part of blood) from the animals' other blood components (such as clotting factors). The next step, of course, was to inject some of this antitoxin into other animals and then to give them a dose of diphtheria bacteria to see if it prevented or stopped the progress of the disease. Von Behring conducted this experiment, injecting guinea pigs, horses, and dogs first with antitoxin and later with the diphtheria bacteria. None of the experimental animals who had gotten the antitoxin became ill with diphtheria. Von Behring had found a new way to prevent diseases whose deadly effects were caused by poisons. In 1901, von Behring was awarded the Nobel Prize in Medicine.

Meanwhile, back in Paris, Roux and his team were administering the antitoxin to French children. At a medical conference in 1894, Roux announced that because of the new antitoxin, the death rate from diphtheria among infected Parisian children had declined from 56% to 24%. When the doctors at the conference heard this wonderful news, the hall erupted in cheers and the doctors threw their hats in the air in celebration. Diphtheria, which had previously killed tens of thousands of children every year, would soon become a very rare disease. By 1913, a diphtheria antitoxin was perfected and made available to all.

In the years that followed, researchers developed antitoxins to combat a number of diseases. Tetanus was one of the main targets of this research. Tetanus is caused by spores produced by tetanus bacilli (*Clostridium tetani*). The spores, which remain viable in soil (or on pavements or other exposed surfaces) enter open wounds, such as cuts and scrapes. Sometimes also called lockjaw, tetanus causes intense, often violent, muscle spasms and muscle rigidity (especially of the jaw—hence its common name). Research based on von Behring's work eventually led to the development of a tetanus antitoxin.

Why Vaccines Work

Though Louis Pasteur, Emil von Behring, and other dedicated medical researchers were delighted that their vaccines and antitoxins prevented disease, they would all have admitted that they really had no idea *why* they worked. At that time, very little was known about the **immune system**—the body system whose job is to attack and kill "alien" invaders, such as pathogens, in the body. The development of vaccines and the need to know how and why they worked led to tremendous advances in medical understanding of the immune system.

Soon after the discovery of antitoxins, scientists understood that both they and vaccines produced some type of disease-fighting reaction in the body. They suspected that vaccines activated disease-fighting cells, which they dubbed **antibodies**. How or why antibodies worked remained a mystery. Finding the solution to this puzzle obsessed German doctor and biochemist Paul Ehrlich. Unlike most other biologists working in the early years of the twentieth century, Ehrlich felt that the key to solving this problem lay in chemistry. His years of studying the interaction between toxins and antibodies led him to believe that they had some sort of complex chemical relationship with each other. At that time, chemistry was a field that concentrated mainly on chemical reactions among nonliving substances. Ehrlich set out to show that chemistry ruled some biological functions, as well. He grew pathogens and toxins in lab dishes and tested a wide variety of chemicals to see which killed or neutralized

Figure 4.1   German doctor and biochemist Paul Ehrlich, who survived a bout with tuberculosis, conceived the idea of a "magic bullet," a concept wherein a chemical substance could selectively target a bacterium without affecting other organisms.

them. Because of this work, Ehrlich became known as the founder of the field of immunochemistry. His research also led him to a hypothesis about antibodies that was revolutionary for its time.

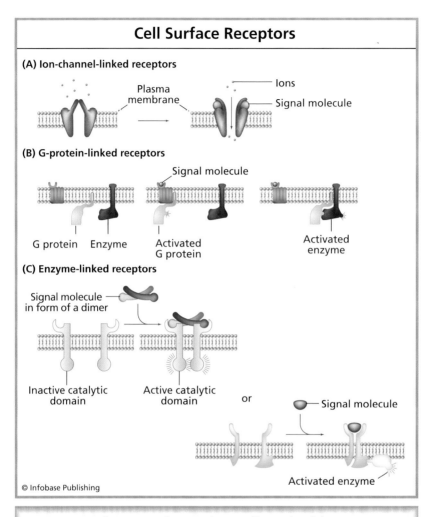

Cell Surface Receptors

(A) Ion-channel-linked receptors

Plasma membrane

Ions

Signal molecule

(B) G-protein-linked receptors

Signal molecule

G protein   Enzyme

Activated G protein

Activated enzyme

(C) Enzyme-linked receptors

Signal molecule in form of a dimer

Inactive catalytic domain

Active catalytic domain

or

Signal molecule

Activated enzyme

© Infobase Publishing

Figure 4.2 This picture shows only a small sample of the many types of receptors found on the outer surface of cells. The cell receptors are made from specific arrangements of proteins. In image B, a nutrient carried by the blood is shown as being ready to bind to the enzyme. The binding site in the nutrient matches the proteins in the receptor. This matching is the reason that they can bind together.

At a speech before the Royal Society (of scientists) in London in 1900, Ehrlich described his theory of how antibodies work. Ehrlich explained to the assembled scientists that antibodies are related to **receptors** on the surface of cells. Ordinarily, cells use these receptors to recognize the nutrients they need in order to function. Ehrlich stipulated that cells have different receptors for recognizing different types of nutrients and that the cells can distinguish needed nutrients from harmful substances that may pass by in the blood. When a receptor on the cell's surface recognizes a nutrient, the nutrient binds to that particular receptor. Then the receptor lets the nutrient into the cell. Ehrlich explained that this process must involve a chemical relationship, such that the chemicals in the cell receptor must recognize and bind to chemicals in the nutrient. In the same way, Ehrlich explained, chemicals on the surface of a microbe bind to receptors on a cell's surface. Of course, the microbe mimics a nutrient and will kill the cell once it's allowed inside.

Ehrlich suggested that when cells were swamped by microbes, they would start producing many copies of the cell receptor targeted by the microbe. They would shed these extra cell receptors into the bloodstream, where they would become antibodies. The antibodies in the blood would be able to bind to the microbes before the microbes had a chance to bind to a cell. Ehrlich's concept of a "lock and key" relationship between cell receptors, pathogens, and antibodies was revolutionary and would later be proved correct. However, his theory had one significant drawback that would be challenged in the future. Ehrlich's model seemed to imply that all antibodies somehow already existed in the body's cells, which somehow "knew" and recognized the chemistry of the countless disease microbes that might attack them.

This problem was highlighted by Austrian physician and biochemist Karl Landsteiner. Landsteiner enjoyed nothing more than changing the structure of microbes and then observing how body cells grown in a lab dish responded to the weirdly shaped attackers. Specifically, Landsteiner loved altering the combinations of proteins on the surface of a microbe. He knew that it is the microbe's surface proteins that bind to cell receptors and that initiate production of antibodies, which are also proteins. These microbe proteins are called the **antigen**, or the part of the microbe that initiates an immune response. No matter how Landsteiner fiddled with an antigen, no matter what weird combination of proteins he gave it, the body cells in the lab dish were able to form antibodies against it. Landsteiner even created antigens that don't exist in nature. Still, the body cells were able to form antibodies to fight them. Landsteiner had shown that one part of Ehrlich's model was incorrect. Cells had no previous "knowledge" of the chemistry of an attacking antigen. Somehow, some way, cells were able to create antibodies to fight antigens they had never "seen" before.

Landsteiner's theory came to be known as the instructionalist theory of immunity. According to this theory, introduced antigens "instructed" cells to make antibodies to fight them. Instructionalist theory had two basic problems. First, it could not explain why cells did not form antibodies against the body's own **proteins**; that is, it couldn't explain how antibodies were able to distinguish "self" from "non-self." Second, this theory could not account for antibody "memory"; that is, it could not explain why some antibodies created to fight a particular pathogen remained in the body to fight that pathogen whenever it re-invaded. This reaction is called **immune memory**, and it's what people mean when they say they are immune to a disease they've already had.

For nearly 30 years, these problems remained unsolved. The key to solving them lay in the structure of proteins and in the genetic code. By the mid-1950s, technological and medical advances proved that proteins are three-dimensional, folded structures whose shape cannot be altered by contact with cells or other proteins. Protein structure is, in fact, determined by **genes**, or specific sequences of **DNA**. Changing the structure of a protein would be like a person changing the shape of an arm or leg. It is impossible. New discoveries about genes made it absolutely clear that the body must have the innate ability to generate protein-based antibodies to fight the thousands or millions of different antigens they might come into contact with. In other words, the body must be born with genes that create an immune system that can produce antibodies to combat whatever antigens infect it.

DECIPHERING THE IMMUNE SYSTEM

The first scientist to observe the immune system at work was Elie Metchnikoff. This Russian biologist, who some thought partly "mad," had throughout the 1880s been studying the larvae, or immature form, of starfish. While peering into his microscope one day, he noticed some cells attacking a starfish **larva**. He watched, amazed, as a host of larva cells moved quickly toward the attacking cells and began pulling them apart and gobbling them up. Any foreign particle Metchnikoff injected into the starfish larvae were also devoured by these larval cells. Metchnikoff called these defensive cells **macrophages**, or "big eaters." He later discovered other types of cells that also "ate" intruders. Metchnikoff dubbed all these cell defenders **phagocytes**.

Metchnikoff was the first scientist to discover and name cells that are part of the **innate immune system**. The innate, or natural, immune system is the body's first line of defense against pathogens and other invaders. When a pathogen enters the body, infected cells send out a protein alarm signal that calls in the macrophage troops. The macrophages use chemicals to dissolve and destroy the intruder. If the macrophages can't mop up the invaders themselves, they use a chemical signal to activate **natural killer cells**, which attack the pathogens with even stronger chemicals. Most of the time, macrophages and natural killer cells can wipe out the intruders. The cells of the innate immune system are non-specific; that is, they will fight any invader that enters the body. Sometimes it takes more specific and powerful cells to fight an infection. In these cases, the cells of the innate immune system call in the big guns: the cells of the **acquired immune system**.

The acquired immune system's cells are called **lymphocytes**, and many circulate in the body's lymphatic system. **T cells** are one type of powerful lymphocyte. **B cells** are the lymphocytes that are involved in the production of antibodies. Australian immunologist F. Macfarlane Burnet showed how B cells and antibodies work. Burnet asserted that the body must have some cells that are dedicated to the production of antibodies. He stated that each antibody-producing cell would be able to produce only one type of antibody. Burnet suggested that the antibody-producing cells—B cells—would travel through the body with a sample of their particular antibody, or set of proteins, on "display." When a B cell encountered an antigen that had the same or a very similar set of proteins, the B cell would bind to the antigen. Then the B cell would do two things. It would begin making and secreting lots of antibodies (the specific proteins to fight the antigen), and it would begin to reproduce. The B cell would make countless identical copies—or **clones**—of itself. All the clones would be able to destroy their particular antigen. Burnet's idea, known as the clonal selection

The Immune System

The human immune system is a complex system of biological structures and processes within a person that—when working optimally—protects against disease by identifying and killing pathogens (viruses, bacteria, and other infectious agents) and tumor cells. Identifying these pathogens can be difficult for the immune system because they may evolve rapidly in order to develop adaptations for survival so they can ultimately infect their hosts (humans). For example, different strains of flu emerge every year and the human body may not recognize these pathogens as being similar to those of the past year's flu.

The diagram shows some of the body organs that are involved in either making or storing immune system cells. Most immune system cells travel through the body via the **lymphatic system**, which resembles the circulatory system in its extent.

What follows is an overview of some of the immune system cells:

- First Responders: Innate Immune Cells
  - Macrophages
  - Natural killer cells (produced mainly in bone marrow and the spleen)
- Specialists: Acquired Immune Cells
  - Lymphocytes (made in bone marrow, often stored in lymph glands)
  - B cells (produce antibodies)
  - T cells (stored in the thymus gland):
    - Helper T cells (which sample antigen and sound an alarm)
    - Killer T cells, the most powerful microbe killers in the body

Immune System

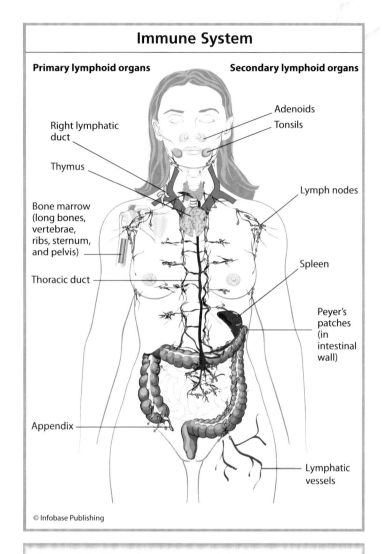

Primary lymphoid organs

Secondary lymphoid organs

Adenoids

Tonsils

Right lymphatic duct

Thymus

Lymph nodes

Bone marrow (long bones, vertebrae, ribs, sternum, and pelvis)

Thoracic duct

Spleen

Peyer's patches (in intestinal wall)

Appendix

Lymphatic vessels

© Infobase Publishing

Figure 4.3   The primary organs of the immune system include the bone marrow and the thymus, where immune-active cells are made or mature. The secondary organs, including the tonsils, adenoids, spleen, and lymph nodes, are sites where immune-active cells attack and destroy foreign materials.

theory of antibody production, is still accepted today. Burnet won a Nobel Prize for his theory, which states the following:

1. B cells exist solely for the production of antibodies.
2. Each B cell is dedicated to the production of only one antibody. Though each cell is capable of producing different antibodies, the proteins it displays on its surface are generated randomly. If any of its surface proteins are activated by an antigen, the B cell will begin producing that antibody.
3. When a B cell binds to an antigen, it will begin producing antibodies and start making clones of itself. Each B cell clone will have an antibody to that one antigen. These B cells will live on for some time in the body and confer immunity to that specific antigen.
4. Any B cell clones that react with "self" molecules (molecules and cells belonging to the body) will be destroyed.

Burnet's brilliant theory was supported by later discoveries in genetics. Geneticists found that B cells are not created from a fixed pool of antibody genes that limit the randomness of their displayed proteins. Instead, the immune system is infinitely flexible. It allows each B cell to assemble proteins for its own antibody display in any way it "wants" to. In other words, antibodies are created "from scratch" and without any genes programming their construction. In fact, the genes that control the immune system make sure that this process is totally random. The immune system is the only body system known in which some of its cells are allowed—in fact, required—to build their own proteins any way they "want." B cells have so much freedom in assembling their antibody proteins that the immune system's genes allow them to create millions of new antibody combinations every *hour* throughout a person's life.

What system could be more "ingenious" in readying itself to fight whatever newfangled pathogen may come its way? In a sense, Ehrlich was right—antibodies for each pathogen do already exist in the body; however, they exist only potentially, not actually. The true workings of the immune system are far more complex and elegant than Ehrlich could ever have imagined.

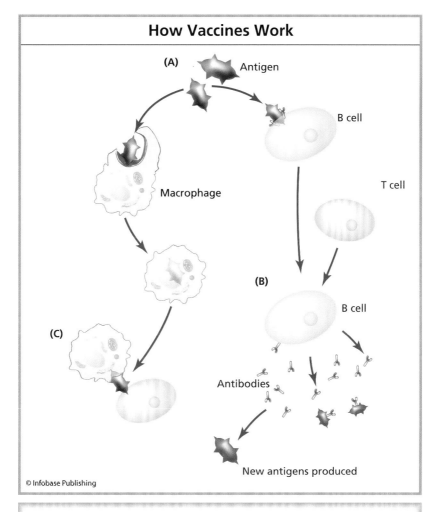

Figure 4.4   (A) A vaccine containing harmless antigens is introduced into the body. (B) B cells, with help from T cells, are stimulated to make antibodies that will fight the weak or dead viruses in the vaccine. The immune system is now able to destroy stronger viruses, if they are introduced. (C) When new antigens enter the body, white blood cells called macrophages engulf them, process the information contained in the antigens, and send it to the T cells so the immune system can fight the introduction of new antigens.

VACCINES AND ANTIBODIES

It now becomes clear how vaccines work. An antigenic part of a pathogen is injected into the body in a vaccine. The antigen encounters a

B cell that is displaying some of the same proteins it has. The B cell binds to the antigen, releases lots of antibodies, and begins reproducing zillions of antibody clones that are specifically designed to destroy this particular pathogen. For as long as the antibody clones remain in the body, the vaccinated person is immune to the disease the vaccine was created to fight.

Researchers soon learned how to perfect the techniques for preparing the attenuated vaccines (e.g., for smallpox) and the killed pathogen vaccines (e.g., for flu) already discussed. As vaccine research progressed and new discoveries about the immune system were made, new types of vaccines were developed. Researchers found that sometimes different parts of a pathogen—different antigenic bits—were more effective at eliciting an immune response and creating antibodies than other parts. Scientists began to make vaccines using the tiniest bits of an antigen to make the safest vaccines possible (vaccines that would not cause the disease they were intended to prevent). These new vaccines owe their existence to advances in genetic engineering.

A **recombinant vaccine** is one in which genetic engineers have removed the inner, disease-causing part of the pathogen, leaving only the outer envelope of the microbe. The intact surface of the pathogen still contains its signature proteins, or antigen. Once it is injected into the body, the antigen initiates the production of antibodies. Thus, even if a pathogen is a harmless "empty envelope," the presence of the surface protein antigen is sufficient to activate

Table 4.1 Examples of Types of Vaccines

Vaccine Type	Infectious Disease
Killed pathogen vaccine	polio (Salk), cholera, influenza, whooping cough (pertussis), typhoid, rabies
Live, attenuated pathogen vaccine	tuberculosis, typhoid, polio (Sabin) cholera, yellow fever, measles/mumps/rubella, chickenpox
Subunit vaccines	tetanus, diphtheria, cholera, meningitis, typhoid, pneumonia, hepatitis B

Note that there is more than one vaccine for some diseases.

Source: Adapted from Open University. Online: http://labspace.open. ac.uk/mod/resource/view.php?id=168412&direct=1.

B cells to make antibodies against the antigen and the disease it causes. A recombinant vaccine against hepatitis B has been in use since 1986.

Most new vaccines are **subunit vaccines**, so called because they are made from tiny snippets of antigen. Subunit vaccines usually consist of bits of antigenic bacteria and sugars that are put together in specific combinations, depending on the disease they're intended to fight. New vaccines against typhoid and pneumonia are made from the cell walls of their particular bacterial pathogens. Researchers have found that even a few proteins from a non-disease-causing part of a pathogen act as antigens and are able to generate antibodies.

Artificial vaccines are made without any pathogens at all. Biologists are now able to string together the correct number and type of amino acids (the building blocks of proteins) to make a protein that is identical to one on the surface of a microbe. When the artificial vaccine is injected into the body, its proteins generate antibodies against the disease pathogen it is mimicking. With artificial vaccines, there is no risk that the vaccination will cause the disease because the pathogen is never used.

New live-virus vaccines are built up out of a few, non-harmful viral genes. These vaccines are called **viral chimeras** (*kiy MEER uhz*), or ghost viruses, because they contain only the fewest possible

Electron Microscopes

An electron microscope works by focusing a beam of electrons (negatively charged atomic particles) at the object being viewed. The electrons are "shot" out of an electron "gun" at very high speeds. Instead of the glass lenses found in light microscopes, the electron microscope uses electromagnetic lenses to control the electron beam. A condenser aperture (opening) is adjusted to focus the image of the object being viewed. When the electrons strike the object, its electrons are affected. Changes in the object's electrons are projected through the electromagnetic lens to form a high-resolution image.

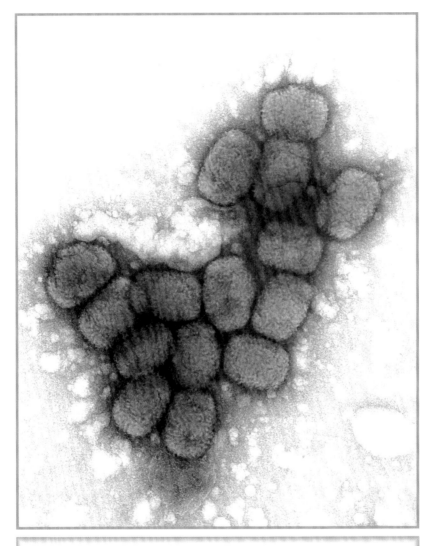

Figure 4.5 This transmission electron micrograph shows smallpox viruses using a negative stain technique.

genes from the pathogenic virus. This "genetic backbone" is then modified by adding to it genes from harmless viruses. The vaccine still contains enough antigenic protein for these viral chimeras to activate B cell production of antibodies against the viral disease, such as dengue fever.

ABOUT VIRUSES

Bacteria can be seen under a normal light microscope. Yet it was not until the 1930s, when the electron microscope was invented that scientists were able to see the strange "creatures" that we call viruses. The best light microscopes can magnify an object 2,000 times. A modern electron microscope can enlarge an object up to 2 million times. Because viruses are thousands of times smaller than bacteria, no one had seen a virus before they peered into an electron microscope.

Once they could see viruses, scientists were better able to study them. Researchers were—and still are—amazed at how strange viruses are. For example, viruses are not living things—though they are not dead either. On their own, viruses can do none of the things organisms can do: They have no respiration or metabolism; they can't move around; and they can't reproduce. They seem to be no more than non-living "stuff." Yet when viruses come into contact with and enter living cells, the viruses are transformed. It is inside living cells that viruses can fulfill their only purpose for being—reproduction. Once inside a cell, a virus hijacks the cell's genes that control reproduction. The virus forces the cell to reproduce viral DNA instead of cell DNA. In this way, each cell creates numerous copies of the virus. In some cases, all these viral clones kill the cell. In other cases, the virus controls its rate of reproduction to keep the cell alive and serving its needs. In a word, viruses are the ultimate parasites.

Although there are many theories about the evolution of viruses, no one really knows how they evolved. Some scientists believe that viruses—which are no more than a collection of genes and proteins—broke away from living cells many millions of years ago. Somehow, these protein "things" learned how to survive in a totally dormant (inactive) state until they found living cells to infect.

5

Fighting Fear: The Battle Against Polio

With smallpox wiped out in most industrialized nations and with many other childhood diseases having fallen to advances in medicine, one might think that the first half of the twentieth century was a worry-free time, at least in terms of disease. Yet this century saw the resurgence of a disease that probably generated more fear among the general population—particularly parents—than any other. That disease was **polio**.

Polio (its full name is *poliomyelitis*) has likely been plaguing people for millennia. There are pictures from ancient Egypt and ancient healers' accounts of an awful, paralyzing disease from as far back as 1500 B.C. In 1789, a British doctor described an outbreak of a disease that caused "a debility of the lower extremities," and he commented sadly that "nothing [seems] to do any good but irons [braces] to the legs, for the support of the limbs and enabling the patient to walk." For years, doctors thought polio, sometimes also called infantile paralysis, was a disease of the muscles because it mainly affected the body's muscles. As an Italian physician wrote in 1813, "[The paralysis] begins with two or three days of fever, after which one of these [lower] extremities is found quite paralyzed, immobile, flabby, hanging down, and no movement is made when the sole of the foot is tickled." This last symptom should have clued doctors to the true nature of the disease. When the sole of a normal foot is stroked, it moves; this is a reflex that is controlled by the nervous system. Yet until 1840, when the disease was carefully studied by Jacob von Heine, a German doctor, no one had made this connection. Heine's analysis of the symptoms showed that polio was not a muscle disease but "an affection of the central nervous system, namely the spinal cord." Thirty years later, Heine's conclusion was confirmed by French physician Jean-Martin Charcot, who gained renown as the founder of neurology (the study of the nervous system). Charcot examined the spinal cords of people who had died of the disease. Sure enough, his examinations revealed extensive spinal cord damage in all the polio victims.

SANITATION AND SICKNESS

From the start of the Industrial Revolution (c. 1750–1850), hundreds of thousands of people moved from farms to cities to look for work in factories. They were herded together, living in the vilest, filthiest, most run-down, and overcrowded slums imaginable. There was little or no sanitation; human waste flowed in the gutters, often contaminating drinking water. In the 1850s, London's Dr. John Snow had made the connection between water contaminated with human waste and outbreaks of cholera (a deadly disease caused by bacteria). It took a while, but after Snow's discovery, governments began improving sanitation in city slums. Sewers were built to separate waste from sources of drinking water. These improvements went a long way toward reducing most outbreaks of waterborne diseases. Unfortunately—and ironically—they had the opposite effect on the incidence of polio.

Polio is a waterborne disease that, like cholera and typhoid, is transmitted via contamination with human fecal matter. Before sewer systems were built, most infants and very young children living in slums were exposed to polio. Generally, when polio strikes very young children it either does not make them sick at all or makes them only mildly ill with brief flulike symptoms. The infants who contracted this mild form of polio developed immunity against polio; however, once the new sanitation systems were in place, infants were neither exposed to polio nor contracted a mild case of polio. So

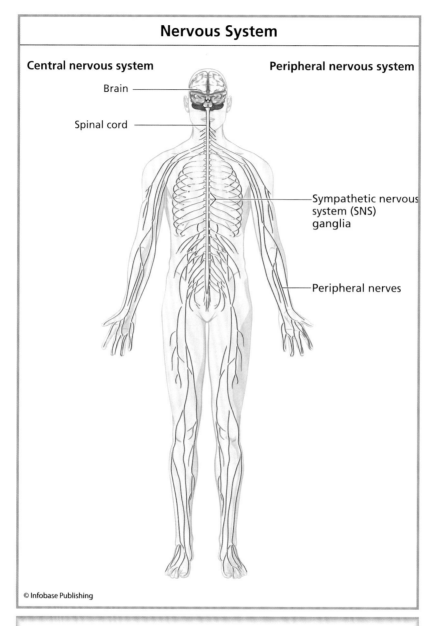

Nervous System

Central nervous system

Brain

Spinal cord

Peripheral nervous system

Sympathetic nervous system (SNS) ganglia

Peripheral nerves

© Infobase Publishing

Figure 5.1 A human's central nervous system consists of the brain and spinal cord, whereas the sensory and ganglionic neurons and the peripheral nerves make up the peripheral nervous system. Notice the large bundles of nerves that emerge from the spinal cord and go to the arms and legs. The parts of the spinal cord attached to these nerves are affected by polio.

the children were at risk of getting more severe and deadly forms of polio when they were older.

The more the cities were cleaned up, the more outbreaks of polio were reported. In the latter part of the nineteenth century, significant outbreaks were reported in Oslo and other cities in Norway. Stockholm, Sweden, and other Scandinavian cities also reported many cases. A serious epidemic occurred in Vermont in 1894, killing 13% of its victims. At this time, no one knew very much about what caused the disease or how a person caught it. A doctor who treated many polio patients in Scandinavia reported that he was certain that the disease was not **contagious**—that it could not be transmitted from person to person. He couldn't have been more wrong. This incorrect notion became part of accepted medical "wisdom" and, for the next 35 years, was one of the main obstacles to finding a way to prevent the disease.

It was not until 1899 that a German physician, Ivar Wickman, proved that polio was, in fact, highly contagious. Wickman was treating patients during yet another polio outbreak in Sweden. Wickman kept meticulous records of every single case of polio that he came across. Unlike the doctors before him, Wickman also recorded information about the mild, non-paralyzing polio cases he saw. This information provided the key to his eventual discovery. By carefully examining patients, Wickman discovered that many people who complained of simple flulike symptoms—headache, fever, nausea—actually had a mild form of polio. By tracking these cases, Wickman discovered that the disease was transmitted by patients with mild polio to others who might come down with the severe, paralyzing form of the disease. Only by correctly diagnosing mild polio and keeping people with this form of the disease away from others could epidemics be prevented. Wickman's discovery went a long way toward limiting the transmission of polio.

WHAT IS POLIO?

Polio is a disease caused by a virus. The polio virus is passed from person to person through contact with human feces that contains the virus. The virus enters the body through the mouth when a person ingests some substance that is contaminated with the virus. Most often, people contract polio from contaminated drinking water, but they also can get it when they swim in contaminated water. Contact with a person who has polio, or with food or an object that has been touched by an infected person can also transmit polio. Once it is inside the body, the polio virus reproduces in cells in the throat and the intestines. In most people, the virus does not spread from the intestines to any other part of the body, so the form of the disease is mild.

The first symptoms of polio are very much like flu. Fever, headache, and nausea occur between 4 and 14 days after infection. Most people are lucky, and these are the only symptoms they ever have. In these patients, the disease is gone within a week or two—but the virus is expelled in their feces. How intensely the human immune system responds to the polio infection determines how severe the disease will be. In only 2% of cases does a person come down with the severe form of paralytic polio. Between 80% and 90% of patients who get paralytic polio are children.

In paralytic polio, the virus travels from the intestines to the spinal cord. The infection is so intense that lesions form on the spinal cord where the virus has infected and killed nerve cells, or **neurons**. The spinal cord is the go-between that sends and receives messages between the brain and the body. The polio virus specifically attacks those nerve cells in the spinal cord—called motor neurons—that affect body movement. When **motor neurons** are destroyed, the parts of the body whose movement they control become paralyzed. In polio, though the neurons that control movement in the body's muscles are destroyed, the nerve endings in the affected muscles continue to function. Polio causes the affected muscles to repeatedly cramp, or to go into spasms. Because the nerves in the muscles are still functioning, these spasms are incredibly painful. Polio wards resounded with the cries of children in terrible pain. Doctors were advised not to give polio sufferers any painkillers for fear that they would weaken the muscles that enabled the patient to breathe. Thankfully, this painful period occurred only during the early stages of the illness.

DREADING SUMMER

Polio strikes mainly during the warm months of the summer. The first major outbreak in the United States began in New York City in

July 1916. By the time the epidemic had run its course, more than 27,000 people had been infected and 7,000 had died. Sadly, many New Yorkers, and others, blamed newly arrived immigrants for bringing the disease. Medical professionals quickly showed that they had not. Yet prejudice against immigrants was strong, and some ugly incidents occurred in New York.

People's feelings of helplessness led them to take drastic measures to combat the disease. The mayor of New York imposed a strict **quarantine** on those infected. Police or health workers forcibly took infected babies and children from their mother's arms and carried them away to quarantine hospitals, where no visiting was allowed. Some New Yorkers who survived this quarantine describe the overwhelming fear they felt as children when they were snatched from their homes and kept in a huge hospital ward where they didn't see their parents for weeks or months.

The quarantine was a desperate—and ineffective—measure. It did not stop the spread of the disease because the role that mild forms of polio played in its transmission was not yet fully understood. More desperate measures were taken: Stray animals were captured and destroyed, and pets were confiscated and killed in case they had transmitted polio. (They hadn't.) Panicky people came up with the most outlandish ideas about how polio spread. Some said it was spread by sharks that swam across the ocean and breathed out polio viruses they'd picked up in Europe. Others claimed that tarantulas (large spiders) injected the virus into bananas imported into the United States from the tropics. A few even insisted that the invisible waves coming from the newfangled radios caused and transmitted polio. Needless to say, none of these weird ideas was right.

Polio outbreaks continued to occur on and off for years. Some outbreaks were brief and infected few. Others were more widespread. None was as devastating as the epidemic that hit during the summer of 1952. Swimming pools, theaters, schools, summer camps, and even churches closed down to stop the spread of the disease. Parents kept their children indoors all summer, fearing that letting them go outside to play would expose them to polio. Hospitals were full to bursting. One nurse described how "there were 16 or 17 new admissions every day. You'd hear a child crying for someone to read to him . . . or to explain why she can't move. It was an atmosphere of grief, terror, and helpless rage. It was horrible."

Nearly 58,000 cases of polio ended up killing 3,000 people and paralyzing thousands more. Polio most often paralyzed the legs, but sometimes the arms were affected, too. The most dreaded form of the disease also paralyzed the muscles in the chest that enable a

The Secret Pain of Franklin Delano Roosevelt

Franklin Delano Roosevelt was born into one of the wealthiest families in America. In the summer of 1921, when Roosevelt was 39 years old, he was vacationing with his family in Canada. In August, he began to feel ill but shrugged the feeling off as overwork. (He had been running [unsuccessfully] for vice president of the United States.) One night, Roosevelt experienced chills, and by the next morning he found that his right knee and leg were too weak to support him. By evening, his left leg was equally weak. Soon he couldn't stand up and could hardly breathe. His wife, Eleanor, first called a local doctor who did not diagnose polio because of Roosevelt's age. The doctor prescribed strong massages to strengthen the weak muscles. The massages were agonizing. Still, Roosevelt's condition worsened, with paralysis spreading to his arms and hands. Eleanor called in a specialist who correctly diagnosed polio. The doctor stated gravely that Roosevelt would probably be permanently paralyzed.

Despite being in constant pain, Roosevelt showed a cheerful face to his family. He did not want to worry his young children. He underwent painful treatments and exercises and, by 1922, his arms and torso were no longer paralyzed. Yet he never walked again and spent the rest of his life in a wheelchair. Roosevelt certainly did not let his disability dampen his ambition. He became a leader of the Democratic Party and, in 1932, was elected president of the United States. The media never sensationalized his disability. When Roosevelt appeared in public, the press

person to breathe. People who could not breathe had to be placed in an iron lung, a machine that helped them breathe. Some patients had to spend months or years lying on their back in an iron lung until—with therapy—they could breathe on their own. Children

Figure 5.2   This is one of only two photographs of Franklin Delano Roosevelt in a wheelchair after he had contracted polio. Here, Roosevelt holds his Scotch terrier, Fala, on his lap as he talks to Ruthie Bie, the daughter of one of the caretakers at his Hyde Park, New York, estate.

photographed him only from the waist up so as not to show him in a wheelchair. Of more than 35,000 photos of him as president, only two show him in his wheelchair.

In 1938, Roosevelt created the National Foundation for Infantile Paralysis, later known as the March of Dimes. The group raised a great deal of money to help victims of polio and to fund research into finding a way to prevent or cure the disease.

The Iron Lung

The iron lung was invented in 1927 by Philip Drinker, an engineer who worked at Harvard University's School of Public Health. The iron lung was a hollow metal cylinder that had holes in it so that doctors and nurses could reach the patient inside. The machine was connected to a pump that changed the air pressure inside the iron lung. First, the pump created a vacuum inside the tank, and the vacuum caused the patient's lungs to expand and take in air, or inhale. When the pump relaxed, the vacuum was no longer created, and the patient's lungs emptied of air, or exhaled. The pump worked continuously creating and releasing the vacuum that kept the patient breathing.

Figure 5.3 This August 16, 1955 image of the emergency polio ward at Haynes Memorial Hospital in Boston, Massachusetts, was taken at a time when the city's polio epidemic hit a high of 480 cases. The critical patients are lined up close together in iron lung respirators so that a team of doctors and nurses can give fast emergency treatment as needed.

found the iron lung terrifying. One little girl remembered how frightened she was seeing other children in her ward in iron lung machines. "Only their heads stuck out of this big, white machine," she said. "I thought they didn't have bodies." She had nightmares about these life-saving machines for years.

A child who survived paralytic polio often had to undergo several operations to correct deformities in the affected limbs. Often one leg was shorter than the other, or a foot was malformed. Even with these corrective surgeries, many victims had to walk wearing heavy leg braces and using crutches for the rest of their lives.

THE SEARCH FOR A VACCINE

It goes without saying that medical researchers in the 1950s were desperate to find a vaccine to prevent polio. Their search for a vaccine was built on important medical discoveries made earlier. For example, early in the century physicians Karl J. Landsteiner and Erwin Popper discovered that polio was caused by a virus, which they were able to culture in the lab. In 1910, Dr. Simon Flexner of the Rockefeller Institute for Medical Research developed a type of polio vaccine that was made from live virus mixed with **serum** (a part of blood) taken from recovering polio patients. The vaccine was only partly successful. Two vaccines—one containing attenuated virus and the other killed virus—were tested in the mid-1930s. Neither vaccine worked well. The killed-virus vaccine was quickly withdrawn after its initial trials because of as-yet undisclosed side effects. Why didn't any polio vaccine work? It was a mystery that frustrated scientists.

The next advance in developing a polio vaccine came from researchers at Harvard University who found a way to overcome the problem of mass-producing the virus for a vaccine. Before John Enders, Thomas Weller, and Frederick Robbins began their research, polio virus was cultured in nerve cells—their natural "habitat." Unfortunately, vaccines that are derived from nerve cells often cause severe allergic reactions in the people who get the vaccine. So another way to grow the virus had to be found. In 1948, the three Harvard scientists successfully cultured large amounts of polio virus from monkey kidney cells. Vaccine made from these cells produced

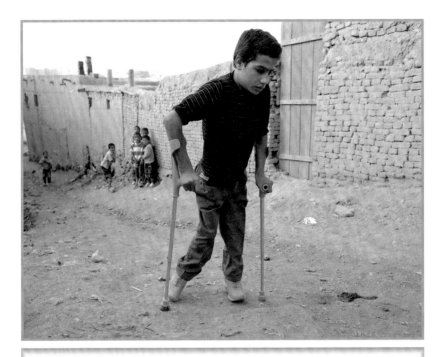

Figure 5.4   Polio is still a problem in some parts of the world. Here, Fawad Rahmani, 11, makes his way home using his crutches and special braces fitted from the International Committee of the Red Cross Orthopedic Clinic on September 26, 2009 in Kabul, Afghanistan. Fawad has had polio since he was two years old.

no allergic reaction in people. The researchers won the Nobel Prize for their discovery.

Still, one unavoidable and nagging question remained: Why did earlier vaccines made from viruses taken from polio victims not confer immunity on those who were vaccinated? Some scientists started to wonder if there was more than one strain of polio virus and if a vaccine had to include all the strains for it to be effective.

The Salk Vaccine

In 1948, scientists with the March of Dimes undertook an all-out effort to find all the strains of polio virus that infected humans. One of the lead scientists in this Typing Program was Dr. Jonas Salk. Salk was a bacteriologist (a scientist who studies bacteria) who was also very interested in viruses. He was doing research on the influenza virus when he was invited to join the Typing Program team. The work was tedious, but necessary. Typing Program scientists had to screen more than 100 different strains of polio to determine if they fit into one of the three types of polio virus the researchers thought existed. Though under extreme pressure to produce a result, the soft-spoken Dr. Salk maintained a cool, professional attitude and continued to work methodically and as quickly as possible. He improved on the March of Dimes' laborious method of typing and devised a far quicker typing system. By 1951, Salk's research team had identified the three types of polio virus. The way was cleared for incorporating them into an effective vaccine. Salk and his team immediately began to work on developing a vaccine. Unfortunately, it could not be perfected in time to prevent the suffering of 1952.

Figure 5.5 Dr. Jonas E. Salk, pictured at age 38 as a professor of research bacteriology at the University of Pittsburgh, is shown in a laboratory on March 27, 1954, as assistant Ethel J. Bailey works on a step in the vaccine's production.

Salk preferred vaccines using killed viruses. First, though, he had to grow live viruses, which he did using the Harvard method. Then he killed the polio viruses by mixing them with formalin. Salk and his team created many vaccine formulas using various combinations of "corpses" of the three virus types. They tested the vaccines in the lab and, in the spring of 1952, were ready to start tests on human subjects. The tests were conducted in secret, using volunteers (mostly prisoners). Blood was taken from polio victims, the virus type was

The Cutter Incident

National jubilation over the success of the Salk vaccine was marred by what came to be known as the Cutter Incident. People everywhere were so relieved that a vaccine had been found, they demanded that every child in the United States be vaccinated right away. The March of Dimes stated that it would have enough vaccine for 20 million children; however, some doctors claimed that there should be enough vaccine produced to vaccinate 45 million children. Getting this quantity of vaccine ready on time meant that vaccine manufacturers had to work overtime to produce it. The vaccine producers were overwhelmed with orders and with work. They announced that many communities would have to wait for their supply of vaccine. The lack of vaccine became a political issue, with accusations flying about diverting vaccine (to the politically well connected or even to the black market), deliberately slowing up production, or failing to make workable plans to produce the needed amount.

On April 27, 1955, the U.S. Public Health Service (PHS) reported that six cases of paralytic polio had occurred in children inoculated with polio vaccine made by Cutter Laboratories in California. Over the next few days, more cases were reported—all in children vaccinated with the Cutter vaccine. Investigations later showed that the Cutter vaccine contained live virus. At a PHS meeting several days later, identified, and then it was injected into subjects who had already suffered from a different type of polio. When the subjects' blood was tested, it was found to contain antibodies against the type of polio virus in the vaccine. None of the subjects came down with polio. This early success led to larger trials, in 1953, on hundreds of volunteers. Each trial was a success. By this time, the subjects were being vaccinated with all three types of polio virus at once. Each subject then tested positive for all three antibodies.

officials ordered that the vaccination program be continued, but without Cutter vaccine. By this time, the Cutter vaccine had been in use for more than two weeks. Only in May was the mass vaccination program halted. When PHS experts visited all the labs making the vaccine, they shut down two of them. Finally, a commission of polio experts, including Dr. Salk, met to discuss the problem. The members concluded that the method used to make the vaccine had to change to ensure that the vaccine was safe. The initial rule that the Salk vaccine could be bottled in the same plant that cultured live virus was changed. Now, live virus had to be grown in one lab, and the dead virus vaccine had to be bottled in a separate facility. Other safety regulations were put in place: All large samples of vaccine had to be tested for live virus before bottling; the virus-killing process had to be improved; and the bottled vaccine had to be tested again for live virus before it could be used.

Still, after the Cutter Incident, many parents withdrew their children from the vaccination program for fear that they would be infected with live virus. Large segments of the public were torn and did not know what to do. Some people wanted their children to get vaccinated immediately, even though the Cutter Incident slowed down vaccine production; others rejected the whole idea of vaccination.

Some people blamed the PHS for having lax rules and little oversight at the beginning of the program. Whoever was to blame, the Cutter Incident underlines the risks that are always inherent in vaccination.

In the summer of 1954, the March of Dimes began a nationwide vaccination program using the Salk vaccine. Two million children—called the Polio Pioneers—volunteered to get vaccinated. Half the group got the vaccine; the other half got a **placebo** (inactive substance). By the spring of 1955, the results of the test were announced to an anxiously waiting public: "The new Salk vaccine works, is safe, effective, and potent." The public went wild with joy and relief. Salk was celebrated as a savior and a hero. Doctors around the country obtained the vaccine and administered it to their patients. It took only a few years for the effectiveness of the vaccine to be revealed. Polio cases dropped from about 3,200 in 1960 to 910 in 1962.

The Sabin Vaccine

Dr. Albert Sabin was a virus and vaccine specialist who immigrated to the United States from Poland in 1921. During World War II, Sabin helped develop vaccines to prevent U.S. troops from getting dengue fever, hepatitis, and a form of encephalitis (a neurological disease). Sabin had used both killed viruses and attenuated viruses in making the different vaccines. His wartime research led him to conclude that live, attenuated viruses were more effective than killed viruses in a vaccine.

After the war, Sabin worked solely on developing a polio vaccine. He was convinced that an oral vaccine containing attenuated virus would be far more effective than Salk's injectable killed-virus vaccine. Jonas Salk was by then the most celebrated scientist in America, so Sabin got little attention or support for his work from the March of Dimes or other foundations or government agencies that funded polio research. By 1955, Sabin had developed what he believed to be an effective oral polio vaccine. He began testing it on small groups of volunteers (prisoners again), and received positive results. Though the March of Dimes pretty much ignored Sabin's accomplishment, the World Health Organization (WHO) did show interest and started to fund larger trials of the oral vaccine.

In 1957, the WHO funded a program to use Sabin's oral vaccine to vaccinate 4.5 million children living in a part of Russia that was plagued by polio epidemics. The number of polio cases in Russia plummeted. The dramatic success in Russia made it impossible for American polio foundations to ignore Sabin. In 1960, the Sabin oral

Figure 5.6   Dr. Albert Sabin is shown conducting his final research project on May 1, 1969, in a Cincinnati, Ohio, lab. The research was an attempt to link human cancer to viruses.

polio vaccine was approved for use in the United States. Over the next few years, Sabin's oral vaccine became more popular and more widely used than Salk's injectable vaccine. Sabin's vaccine was a liquid dropped onto a sugar cube that a person sucked on and enjoyed; letting a sugar cube dissolve in the mouth was far more pleasant than getting a shot. It was also shown that, in some cases, the Sabin vaccine was more effective than Salk's.

An intense rivalry arose between the two scientists and their supporters about whose vaccine was better. The debate about which was the better vaccine continued until 1997. In that year, the U.S. Centers for Disease Control (CDC) issued a statement about the condition in which each vaccine was most effective. In underdeveloped areas where people still get polio from a "wild" type of virus (a virus that occurs naturally and does not come from another infected person), the Sabin vaccine is most effective. Because it is taken orally, the Sabin vaccine blocks virus replication in the intestines. In more developed countries, such as the United States, where the wild type of virus has been eradicated, the Salk vaccine is preferred. The Salk vaccine is injected into the bloodstream and, thus, does not aid in killing the virus in the intestines. Today, both vaccines—and both Salk and Sabin—are hailed for their major contributions to halting the spread of one of the most dreaded childhood diseases.

Eradicating Disease

As scientists gained a better understanding of antibodies and the immune system, newer, safer, and more powerful vaccines were developed. Medical researchers worked together to perfect vaccines for a wide variety of diseases. They soon realized that it might be possible to eradicate some diseases altogether. Coordinated by the World Health Organization (WHO), scientists embarked on ambitious projects to eliminate some diseases that had plagued humankind for centuries, such as polio and smallpox. Several thorny problems had to be solved before these global vaccination programs could begin. First, a daunting amount of vaccine had to be produced to vaccinate hundreds of millions of people. The vaccine also had to remain safe and potent while it was being stored and transported to the far corners of the world. Then, of course, there was the matter of who was going to pay for producing, distributing, and administering all of this vaccine. Finally, and most problematic of all, was convincing people from every culture and nation on Earth that getting vaccinated would help, not hurt, them and their children.

THE FIRST BATTLE: ERADICATING SMALLPOX

In 1967, the WHO convened a meeting of public health professionals and infectious disease experts from around the world. The purpose of the meeting was to launch a global program to completely eradicate smallpox, the "ancient scourge" that killed and disfigured millions of people throughout history. An effective vaccine against smallpox was already widely available and in use in rich, developed countries, but it was largely unknown in many undeveloped, poor nations. The task ahead was enormous: to obtain the agreement and cooperation of every government of every country on Earth to allow its population to be vaccinated. The details regarding this massive undertaking were set out in a report produced at the Twentieth World Health Assembly. The Intensified Smallpox Eradication Program (ISEP) set forth the methods that could be used to persuade national leaders and their people of the benefits of smallpox vaccination. The report showed that at least 150,000 health professionals would be needed to implement the program. It also set out a geographical plan and a timetable for ISEP implementation. Above all, the WHO realized that its plan must be flexible and adaptable to fit the cultural and political conditions in each country. Finally, the report detailed how much the program would cost, how much developed countries were expected to contribute, and how much money needed to be raised from private foundations and businesses.

Money was almost always a problem in implementing ISEP. Sufficient funds even to begin the program were not received by the WHO until 1974. The WHO contributed $2.4 million a year from its own budget, but getting developed nations to commit to a generous annual contribution was difficult and frustrating. In most years, officials had to plead for additional funds just to keep the program going. Year after year, they wrangled just enough money from contributors to keep the program alive.

Getting the heads of state of every country on Earth to cooperate with the program was another headache for the WHO. In some places, both leaders and the population were highly suspicious of vaccination. Everyone agreed that eliminating smallpox would be a great accomplishment, but too often, leaders of developing countries were wary of the vaccination's possible side effects, or thought that it might actually cause an epidemic of the disease. Other obstacles blocked smooth implementation of ISEP. In some nations, leaders were happy to have their people vaccinated, but events made widespread inoculation impossible. Civil wars, epidemics of other diseases such as cholera, refugee problems, or simply other national priorities stood in the way of a comprehensive vaccination program. Wars and disease outbreaks altered the geographical vaccination plan—the WHO would have to wait until these problems were resolved. Distrust or other national priorities were tackled with public relations campaigns, education, and sound argument. A WHO handbook was prepared, which explained the smallpox eradication effort in detail. Every head of state and health minister received both the handbook and many personal visits from WHO officials. As each obstacle was overcome, the WHO had to be ready to move in and vaccinate the entire population as quickly as possible.

A goal was set to vaccinate at least 80% to 95% of each nation's population. Doctors and health workers carried out this part of the program. Then a different team of workers conducted an assessment of each nation's program. They checked the number of people vaccinated. If too many people had fallen through the cracks, vaccination teams were called in again to vaccinate those who had been missed the first time around. The assessment team also determined if any vaccinated people had suffered either side effects or the actual disease.

Year after year, the dedicated WHO workers traveled from the crowded slums of teeming Asian and African cities to the smallest villages hidden away in rainforests or dotting vast deserts. With the help of national and local governments, people everywhere in the world were vaccinated against smallpox. In some places, particularly villages in India, the residents were suspicious of the vaccine and resisted having their children vaccinated. WHO officials learned that patience and crafting explanations relevant to local beliefs were the best means of persuasion. Using force or intimidation was usually counter-productive, creating a more stubborn or violent resistance among the local population. Taking the time to persuade people to voluntarily submit to vaccination prolonged ISEP. Yet in December 1979, a WHO commission finally made the announcement that smallpox had been conquered around the globe. Many consider this to be the greatest accomplishment in twentieth-century medicine.

MORE WARS ON DISEASE

After their success in eradicating smallpox, the WHO targeted polio as the next disease to be eliminated globally. In May 1988, the

Figure 6.1 A Nigerian child is immunized during the Smallpox Eradication and Measles Control Program of West Africa in the 1970s. In 1979, the World Health Organization declared the global eradication of smallpox and recommended that all countries cease vaccination.

WHO officially launched its Global Polio Eradication Initiative. This program was similar to ISEP and was organized along similar lines. Teams of health workers descended on developing nations around the world. The success of the smallpox program had led some nations to set aside "national immunization days," when citizens went to local clinics to have their children immunized against polio. In just over a decade (by 2000), more than 550 million children in 82 countries had received the polio vaccine. The success of the program is obvious in the number of polio cases. As reported by the WHO, in 1988, before the program began, there were more than 350,000 cases of polio among the world's children. By 2003, that number had dropped to only 784. Between 1988 and 2004, the incidence of polio had decreased 99% worldwide.

Unfortunately, increasing resistance to vaccination in parts of India and Nigeria had increased the number of polio cases to 1,940 by 2005. These regions sustain wild polio virus, so outbreaks continue

Saving Stockpiles

Once smallpox was eliminated as a global health threat, the question arose about what to do with the smallpox viruses left in some medical laboratories. The WHO strongly urged the labs to destroy these last remnants of this terrible disease. Other scientists were not so sure. They speculated that it was possible that some variant of the smallpox virus might be lurking somewhere on the planet and that having some smallpox virus in storage might help researchers fight the new disease—if it existed. Both doctors and politicians raised the worrying notion that the remaining smallpox viruses could be used in germ warfare; that is, they could be used to make lots more smallpox virus, which might then somehow be released in an enemy country to kill many of its people.

The issue was decided by the two nations that still retained stores, or stockpiles, of smallpox virus: the United States and Russia. Both nations insisted that their virus was stored in well-defended, secure labs so that no one could steal it. Some people remain skeptical, pointing out that a lab worker still might be able to take some virus and sell it to a hostile government or to terrorists. Yet the stockpiles of smallpox virus have remained safe in their secure labs for twenty years. Everyone hopes they stay that way.

Figure 6.2 In this 2000 photograph, the district immunization officer of Gorakhpur, India, administers polio vaccine to a group of children during National Immunization Day.

to occur and sometimes to spread. Still, with intensive and ongoing educational programs, the WHO is hopeful that all forms of polio can be eradicated globally in the 2010s.

The WHO and other global health organizations urged drug companies to develop an inexpensive vaccine to fight meningitis, a disease of the nervous system and brain that is often deadly or severely disabling. College students in the United States and other developed nations are often advised to get a meningitis inoculation before they go to school. Yet the risk of meningitis in developed countries is dwarfed by its devastation in many nations in sub-Saharan Africa. In this region at the onset of the dry season, **meningitis** begins to strike. No one knows why this season brings on the disease. In one of the worst epidemics (1996 to 1997), about 250,000 Africans were infected, and more than 25,000 died of meningitis.

A new, low-cost vaccine has recently been developed to fight meningitis. It is a type of conjugate vaccine, so called because it connects (or conjugates) a sugar to a protein from the bacteria that cause the disease. The new vaccine costs only 50 cents a dose, so African countries are able to help buy the drug for their people. The initial trials of the vaccine have shown promising results, and expanded trials are underway. The WHO hopes to begin inoculating 45 million people a year (until at least 250 million are vaccinated) in the "meningitis belt," which extends from Mali and Burkina Faso to Ethiopia. The leaders in all of the 25 most-affected countries strongly support the effort. It remains for these leaders and the international public health community to convince Africans that the vaccine is safe and that they are not being used as "guinea pigs" to test an unreliable drug. It is understandable that Africans' history of being colonized and ruled by Western nations has made many of them wary of medicines offered by their former colonizers. Slowly but surely, however, increasing numbers of Africans are being persuaded to trust these international efforts.

ENDING CHILDHOOD DISEASES

The success of the polio vaccines encouraged medical researchers to begin the search for vaccines to prevent other potentially dangerous childhood diseases. **Measles** was one of the first diseases to be tackled. Measles is caused by a virus, is highly contagious, and may cause blindness or even death in the most severe cases. Measles primarily strikes children between the ages of 6 and 15. Before 1963, there were between 500,000 and 4 million cases of measles annually in the United States, and 500 children died from the disease each year. The main symptoms of measles are a severe rash covering the body and the eyes' sensitivity to light.

The first measles vaccine was developed by John Enders in 1954, but it took nine more years for the vaccine to be made safe enough for widespread use. In 1963, two different kinds of vaccine were made publicly available: One was made with attenuated virus, and the other contained killed virus. By 1967, public health officials withdrew the killed virus vaccine because it sometimes caused serious side effects and, even more rarely, left the inoculated child vulnerable to wild-type measles.

Children around the United States were vaccinated with the attenuated vaccine, and 95% of them developed antibodies against measles. In the next few years, the number of measles cases in the country dropped dramatically. After the nationwide vaccination program was underway, the number of measles cases dropped by 98%.

The next childhood disease to succumb to vaccination was **mumps**. Mumps is a childhood disease spread by a virus. Its most common symptom is swelling of the salivary glands or other glands in the neck. In children, mumps is not a serious disease. Some

An Unconquerable Foe

Scientists have made remarkable progress in creating vaccines to prevent disease and in developing drugs to fight them. Yet there is one affliction that may never be conquered. It is the most widespread disease of all—the common cold.

The main reason that the common cold may never be outwitted has to do with the many types of viruses that cause it. There are about 300 different viruses that produce cold symptoms. It would be very difficult, if not impossible, for a person to be vaccinated against all 300 viruses. It's equally hard to determine exactly which of these "bugs" is causing one particular bout with a cold. The problem is further complicated by the way the virus acts in the body.

It may seem an odd survival strategy, but cold viruses persist because they allow themselves to be easily destroyed by macrophages and other cells of the innate immune system. The cold viruses enter the body and begin to generate their miserable, well-known symptoms. The innate immune system rushes in to start killing the viruses, but this slaughter takes a few days. Before all the viruses are killed off, the person who has the cold is sneezing his or her head off. Sneezing and coughing spread the cold viruses to other people. Thus, even though the particular viruses in one person's nose may be killed, the virus type survives because it's spread to defenseless victims within range of a sneeze. It's also interesting to note that cold children who get mumps have no symptoms at all. Yet in a very few cases, mumps can infect the nervous system and lead to meningitis. For this reason, scientists felt it was important to vaccinate children against mumps. A vaccine against mumps was licensed for use in 1967. This vaccine, too, was made from attenuated virus.

By the end of the decade, health researchers had perfected a vaccine against **rubella**, also called German measles. (Rubella was called

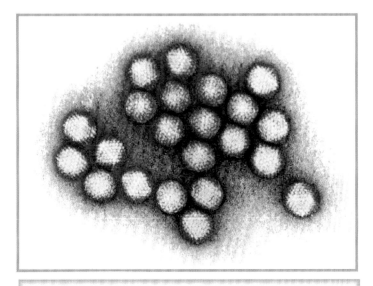

Figure 6.3 This colorized transmission electron micrograph shows adenovirus. It is just one of the 300 different types of viruses that cause the common cold.

viruses are killed by macrophages and the innate immune system before the "big guns" of the acquired immune system need to be called in to battle. For this reason, B cells never get involved in fighting colds. Because cold viruses are so "wimpy" and let themselves be killed so easily, the body never develops antibodies to fight colds. It's an odd but effective strategy that will keep cold viruses vibrant for as long as humans exist.

German measles because it was first described by a German doctor in 1814.) Rubella is a mild viral disease in children. Rubella causes a milder rash than measles and is also far less dangerous. However, rubella has one serious consequence in that if a pregnant woman contracts the virus, it may cause birth defects in her unborn child. For this reason, parents with young daughters used to have "German measles parties." If one girl in the neighborhood had rubella, all her girlfriends would visit her for a party. The purpose of the party was to infect the girls with rubella while they were young. Once a girl has

Shingles

It is true that chicken pox is far less serious in children than in adults. However, once a person has contracted chicken pox, the varicella-zoster virus may stay hidden in the body. The virus hides deep inside nerve cells where the immune system's antibodies can't find it.

If a person is very unlucky, years later the varicella-zoster virus might suddenly and for unknown reasons become activated as herpes zoster virus. The virus causes a painful condition called shingles. Shingles causes blisters, a rash, or chicken pox-like sores on the affected part of the body. Sometimes the sores cause only itching. In severe cases, the infected nerves cause intense pain. Some people with shingles can't even bear the touch of clothing. There is no cure for shingles, but getting antiviral drugs as soon as the condition starts may prevent it from becoming serious. After a period of time, shingles usually disappears as mysteriously as it arrived. The virus goes back into hiding inside nerve cells. It may or may not cause another painful bout of shingles later on. Researchers are currently developing a vaccine to prevent shingles. However, some people have questioned the wisdom of getting a chicken pox vaccination if, though it prevents chicken pox, it will lead to shingles in adulthood.

had rubella, she develops an immunity against it and will not get it when she is older and possibly pregnant. So before the vaccine was developed, parents deliberately tried to infect their daughters with German measles to protect them later in life. Like many other childhood vaccines, the rubella vaccine is made with attenuated virus. Like the other vaccines, at least 95% of vaccinated children develop antibodies against the disease. By the 1970s, these three vaccines were combined and given to young children in one injection, called **MMR** (measles, mumps, rubella).

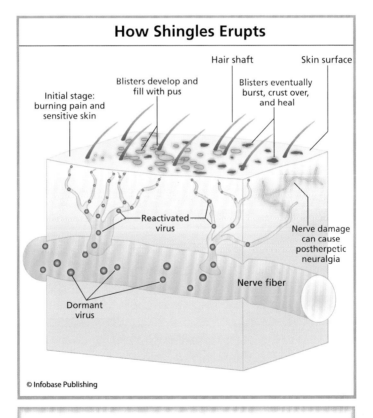

Figure 6.5 Shingles is caused by the varicella-zoster virus, which can live dormant in the nervous system of a person who has had chicken pox, and reactivate under stressful circumstances.

Figure 6.4   This child is shown suffering from mumps in the 1940s. The head wrap was believed to relieve the pressure of swelling.

In 1995, a vaccine to prevent chicken pox was approved for use in the United States. **Chicken pox** is a potentially very serious disease caused by a virus called **varicella-zoster**. Prior to the widespread use of the vaccine, thousands of Americans were afflicted with chicken pox every year. About 11,000 of them became so ill that they had to be hospitalized. About 100 people died of chicken pox annually. Chicken pox produces sores on the skin all over the body. Eventually, the sores disappear, but if a sore scab is removed too early, a lifelong scar will remain. Chicken pox is generally far less

Table 6.1 Schedule of Childhood Immunizations	
Vaccine	Age for Initial Vaccinations
Diphtheria, Tetanus, Pertussis (DTP)	2 months, 4 months, 6 months
Polio	2 months, 4 months
Measles, Mumps, Rubella (MMR)	12–14 months
Varicella (Chicken pox)	12–18 months
* Note that vaccinations for hepatitis A and B, pneumonia, meningitis, and other diseases may depend on whether or not the child is at risk for these diseases. *Source: The Centers for Disease Control, 2009.*	

dangerous in young children than it is in adults. So, like rubella, parents sometimes had (and some still have) "chicken pox parties" for their young sons and daughters. The parents wanted their children to get chicken pox early and develop an immunity to it before they grew up. Today, the chicken pox vaccine is added to the three vaccines previously discussed, and young children get a combination vaccination called **MMPV** (MMR plus varicella).

Whooping cough (also called **pertussis**) is another childhood disease that has been largely eliminated by a vaccine. The pertussis vaccine was first developed in the 1930s. By the 1940s, it was widely used to prevent whooping cough. In 1991, the pertussis vaccine was combined with the vaccines for diphtheria and tetanus. This combination vaccine, called **DTP**, is given to all infants to protect them from these truly serious childhood diseases. DTP is made from inactivated, or killed vaccine, so four shots are generally necessary to immunize the body.

7

Backlash

When the smallpox vaccine first became widely available, some public health officials went a bit overboard in their eagerness to vaccinate citizens. In 1871, the British Parliament passed a Vaccination Act that made vaccination against smallpox compulsory. Anyone who refused to get the smallpox vaccination would be subject to fines, loss of property, or life in the workhouse (a house of correction). In some ways, these were worse punishments than those meted out to hardened criminals. The public and especially the poor were outraged. Some citizens banded together to form the Anti-Vaccination League to fight coerced vaccination. Huge protests were organized, and enraged citizens marched on Parliament. The government, which felt that this response reflected only public ignorance, responded by imposing an even worse condition: Anyone who wanted to get a job had to get a vaccination (and often had to get their children vaccinated, too) before they could work. It was either be vaccinated or starve. The demonstrations and protests increased, sometimes becoming violent.

The British government created a Royal Commission on Vaccination to study the issue. While the commission was doing its work, the anti-vaccination movement gained some important support. The famous writer and playwright George Bernard Shaw became a champion of the protesters. He once compared compulsory vaccination to "burning down London to test a patent fire extinguisher." Other famous and influential people took up the cause. In 1889, the

Royal Commission allowed exemptions from vaccination for "conscientious objectors," though the vaccination program was to continue at full tilt.

Why did so many people, including some very smart and well-educated ones, oppose vaccination so strongly? It is certainly true that the method for mixing up a batch of vaccine was at that time fairly crude. Viruses were sometimes not sufficiently attenuated, and people who got this vaccine often came down with smallpox. In some places, statistics showed that there were more cases of smallpox in areas where the greatest number of people had been vaccinated. Where fewer people were vaccinated, smallpox was much rarer.

The nineteenth-century British revolt against vaccination highlights problems that have plagued vaccines to this day. Creating a safe vaccine is very exacting. The viruses or bacteria in an attenuated vaccine have to be weakened enough so they don't cause the disease they are intended to prevent. Yet they have to be strong enough to generate antibodies. The vaccine must be made with substances that do not spoil over time when they are stored or shipped. These preservatives must be safe and have no negative effects on health. Then there is the issue of the timing of vaccination. Many vaccines today are given to infants—babies less than one year old. Babies get a whole series of vaccinations, which must not harm their tender, young immune systems. One vaccine must not interact with any of the other vaccines that the babies get and make the infants sick or affect their development.

THE DTP PANIC

In 1982, a U.S. television network broadcast a documentary about the dangers of the DTP (diphtheria, tetanus, pertussis) vaccine that all American infants received. The show emphasized the problems associated with the vaccine. The program highlighted infants who had seizures, suffered brain damage and developmental problems, developed severe allergies, and went into shock, among other side effects. After the show aired, people who felt their children, too, had been harmed by the DTP vaccine began to organize. They wanted to find out why their children were harmed and what could be done to make sure vaccines were safe. After doing some research, the parents discovered that the pertussis vaccine was being made with whole virus cells. They began to suspect that it was the whole-cell pertussis vaccine that was overwhelming their children's immune systems and making them ill.

When pressed, public health officials admitted that the whole-cell pertussis vaccine was the most dangerous vaccine given to American infants. Because it was so potent, this vaccine was given in four small doses, at birth and two, four, and six months of age. Many parents questioned whether it was wise to give such a power-ful vaccine to very young children. Doctors countered by pointing out that whooping cough was most often fatal if it struck very young children.

The DTP panic forced into public view the failures of oversight in vaccine production. Parents' organizations found that government agencies charged with ensuring the safety of vaccines were very lax and rarely enforced standards and quality laws. Congressional hearings revealed that some vaccines on the market were totally useless. The hearings brought to light the fact that 75 biologic (living) agents used to make vaccines were not only useless, but dangerous. Yet they had all been licensed and approved by the government. Many doctors were deeply troubled by the revelations about pertussis vaccine, and they testified that in fact they had lost confidence in the ability of government agencies to ensure the safety and effectiveness of the vaccine. Some doctors related that they had reported harmful side effects to government agencies or to the drug companies that made the vaccine. The drug companies were supposed to pass this information on to the Centers for Disease Control (CDC), but they never did. Revealing the harm that their vaccine might cause would hurt profits, so they kept the information to themselves.

By the 1980s, the benefits of vaccines were unquestioningly ac-cepted by most doctors, government health agencies, and all pub-lic health officials. It is likely that their absolute refusal to entertain the notion that vaccines could have terrible, even deadly, side ef-fects fired up the anti-vaccination groups that were gaining strength throughout the country. The research done by parents' groups re-vealed that the pertussis vaccine was still being made using proce-dures developed 30 years earlier. Despite the reported side effects, no effort was made to modernize these procedures. Worse, the

Figure 7.1 Although it has not been scientifically proven, many people believe the early vaccine dosages children are legally required to receive cause development problems, including autism. In this 2005 image, Beau King, 5, from Kailua, Hawaii, who suffers from mercury-related development problems, joins in at a Washington, D.C., rally to protest the use of mercury in vaccines.

government had never established a procedure for tracking reported side effects, so it could not scientifically confirm or deny the claims of harm made by parents.

Anti-vaccination groups hired lawyers to file class-action lawsuits against the drug companies that had produced the pertussis vaccine. The drug companies lost the lawsuits and had to pay many millions of dollars in damages. One by one, the companies stopped making vaccines of any kind. It was just too risky and legally too expensive. To prevent the supply of vaccines from drying up completely, the U.S. government stepped in with a type of "insurance" program to protect the drug companies against lawsuits. For a while, the government even paid the damages awarded by a court to the parents who had sued the companies. With this financial protection from the government, some drug companies began to produce a new form of pertussis vaccine. The acellular pertussis vaccine was made by removing the cell walls from the bacteria and just using some of the inner cell fluid in the vaccine. It was more expensive to produce the acellular vaccine, but doctors thought its greater safety was worth the higher price.

The new acellular vaccine reassured some parents, and the number of babies getting DTP rose again in the 1990s. Yet a new awareness arose among parents. They wondered why they should endanger the lives of their children to vaccinate them against a disease they may never get. Was it worth the risk?

Pertussis vaccine was the subject of intense and widespread research. Researchers concluded that they could not rule out the possibility that some children were harmed by the pertussis vaccine. They also found that 1 in 100,000 children experienced negative effects after getting a DTP shot. Some parents thought that even this risk was too high. Surveys of parents who refused to give their babies DTP shots showed that most of them viewed whooping cough as a disease similar to smallpox. Smallpox vaccination ended when smallpox was

Allergies

Some parents found that after their children received DTP injections, they developed severe allergies. An allergy is an immune system reaction against a particular substance, called an allergen. For example, a child is allergic to chocolate because any chocolate that enters the child's body stimulates the immune system to fight the substances in chocolate. Food allergies most often cause skin rashes or hives. Allergies to airborne particles, such as pollen, usually make a person sneeze. Allergies to chocolate, peanuts, strawberries, or plant pollen—causing hay fever—often have a genetic cause. However, many parents have reported that their allergy-free children developed serious allergies after they'd gotten their DTP shots. Some doctors and medical researchers believe that it is possible that the DTP vaccine might overstimulate a young child's immune system. The overactive immune system might cause the child to develop an allergy.

eradicated. These parents thought that once everyone else's children got DTP shots, their children were safe from pertussis. Alas, this is not the case. Whooping cough is **endemic**, or naturally occurring, in the United States. Thousands of infants and children get whooping cough every year. Often, the disease originates among pre-school children in areas where most parents refuse DTP. Between 1990 and 1999, 18,500 babies, 90% of them unvaccinated, contracted whooping cough, and 93 of them died. In 2003, there were 2,000 cases of whooping cough in the United States, and about 1,400 children had to be hospitalized.

Many school districts in the United States require children to have DTP vaccinations before they can go to school. Yet in areas where most people are still suspicious of vaccines, there is no DTP requirement for school enrollment. In many places, the debate still rages between public health officials who insist that DTP is safe and must be given and parents who are wary of government agencies that, in their view, force them to endanger their children's lives with risky vaccines.

VACCINES AND AUTISM

Leo Kanner is famous as the founder of the field of child psychiatry. In the 1930s and 1940s, Kanner worked at the Johns Hopkins Medical Center in Baltimore, Maryland. During these years, he noted 11 cases of a childhood condition he had never seen or read about before. Kanner noted that the peculiar, even frightening symptoms of this strange condition included a young child's inability to relate to others in normal situations and their seeming to be withdrawn into a "shell" of solitude that enables them to ignore the outside world and other people. Children who have this condition, which Kanner called **autism**, also exhibit strange behaviors such as ongoing repetitive movement (e.g., knocking the head against a wall, rocking), staring at one point for hours, or arranging and ordering objects obsessively. All autistic children are obsessed by things remaining the same, by order and fixed patterns. Some autistic children seem to have remarkable mathematical ability or memory, though many have trouble attaining and using language; others are severely mentally handicapped. There is no cure for autism. Some children may be helped by therapy, but many live out their lives trapped in their strange and awful isolation, eventually nearing "a total retreat into near nothingness." A diagnosis of autism is the start of a lifelong nightmare for the parents of these children.

In the 1970s, it was estimated that about 1 in 2,000 children was autistic. By 2000, the number of autism cases had jumped to about 1 in 200 children—a remarkable and worrying increase. More and more parents became concerned about their children. Some medical professionals spoke of an "epidemic" of autism, but they had no idea what caused it. As the population of parents of autistic children grew, they began researching the problem themselves. They felt that because the number of cases was increasing so dramatically, there had to be an environmental cause of autism. They were determined to find out what it was.

Autism generally first appears when a child is between one and two years old. It is during this time that nearly all children get a

Soldiers as Guinea Pigs?

Since 1998, about 400,000 U.S. soldiers have been given six doses of a vaccine intended to prevent anthrax. The Defense Department believed that the government of Iraq had biological weapons, such as anthrax, that it could use to thwart invading American soldiers. The vaccination program was to protect soldiers against possible biological warfare. Unfortunately, it seems that the vaccine that was used had not been fully tested for side effects. By 2000, more than 500 soldiers reported serious reactions to the vaccine, including dizziness, muscle weakness, joint pain, stomach cramps, and other debilitating symptoms. When these side effects became known, hundreds of soldiers refused to be vaccinated. The Defense Department threatened these soldiers with court-martial (a trial that might land them in a military jail). Some of the soldiers contacted their congressional representatives, and a hearing was held in the House of Representatives. The testimony given at the hearing led the Congress to conclude whole series of vaccinations. In fact, by the time they are two years old, most American children have already received 16 or more vaccinations. It was only natural that the parents of autistic children would want to find out if there was something in any of these vaccines that might be turning their perfectly normal children into autistic strangers. The research done by parents' groups pointed to a substance used in the MMR (mumps, measles, rubella) and sometimes the DTP vaccines as the culprit. The agent is called **thimerosal**, and it is used in vaccines to prevent contamination with bacteria. Though doctors and public health experts vehemently denied this connection, their inability to offer any type of help to autistic children, or any explanation for the cause of the disease, weakened their argument.

Thimerosal is made from ethyl mercury, and mercury is a known neurological toxin that can cause severe neurological and brain damage. Prior to the accusations made by activist parents, no one had

that the Defense Department had forced the soldiers to get a vaccine that had not been sufficiently tested for safety. Further, there was insufficient evidence that the vaccine prevented airborne anthrax. Experts testified that serious side effects from the vaccine occurred at a rate 200 times higher than for a well-tested, safe vaccine.

Six soldiers filed a lawsuit against the Defense Department in 2003. The judge in the case ruled that the U.S. Food and Drug Administration had not followed its own procedures in licensing the anthrax vaccine. The judge also granted any soldier the right to refuse the vaccine without penalty. Despite the ruling, the Army continued to coerce soldiers into getting vaccinated. It was only when the judge threatened Secretary of Defense Donald Rumsfeld with jail that the practice stopped. Many Americans were shocked that the Defense Department would use a poorly tested, ineffective, and potentially harmful vaccine on American troops. It was just one more example of how vaccines could be abused, and the incident increased people's suspicions about vaccines and vaccinations.

Figure 7.2 Most autistic children have difficulty relating to others and to the outside world. Here, Donna Shank interacts with her 7-year-old son, Ryan Shank-Rowe, who has been diagnosed with autism, at their home in Centreville, Virginia, in 2010.

ever thought to calculate how much mercury there was in the MMR and other vaccines. The MMR label, for example, simply showed thimerosal content by weight. At a meeting of vaccine experts in Maryland, one researcher presented calculations that showed that MMR actually contained 25 micrograms (µg) (8.8 x 10 ounces) of ethyl mercury per dose, for a total of 100 µg (3.5 x 10 ounces) in four shots. (Infants who were given hepatitis B vaccinations got an additional 37.5 µg [1.3 x 10 ounces] in these three injections). When the experts checked this amount against the "acceptable and safe" dose of mercury set by the U.S. Environmental Protection Agency (EPA), they were stunned with disbelief. The EPA's limit on the amount of mercury in a newborn's blood was set at 0.1 µg per liter (3.5 x 10 ounces per 1.1 quart) of blood. The EPA did not correlate higher levels of mercury in blood with autism. Yet when the doctors realized that six-month-old infants who were fully vaccinated had gotten as much as 187.5 µg (6.6 x 10 ounces) of ethyl mercury (from MMR,

DTP, and hepatitis B vaccines) injected into them, they could not deny that there might be a connection between the mercury in vaccines and the "epidemic" of autism.

No one knew how long ethyl mercury remained in an infant's body. No one knew if one giant dose of mercury was more or less damaging to the nervous system than continuous, smaller doses, as when pregnant women ate mercury-laden fish. No one knew what happened when both methyl mercury (from fish) and ethyl mercury (from vaccines) combined in the infant's body. In a word, almost nothing was known about this vaccine additive. European health agencies concluded that because of lack of evidence to the contrary, it would be prudent to promote the use of vaccines that do not have thimerosal.

Some public health officials speculated that ethyl mercury might have the same effect on the nervous system and brain as lead. It is known that ingesting even small quantities of lead can lead to brain damage and developmental problems in children. Perhaps the same was true for thimerosal. European health officials banned vaccines with thimerosal in the early 1990s. Yet U.S. health agencies dragged their feet. At one meeting in 1999, agency officials argued against removing thimerosal from vaccines because it would "make them look bad" and appear as if they had not done their job thoroughly. The decision was made to "encourage" drug companies to make their vaccines without thimerosal, but no regulation was enacted to prohibit it. One leading expert, Dr. William Halsey, was upset by the decision. "How," he wondered, "can we say don't eat fish [because it contains mercury] but inject this stuff into babies?"

Parents of autistic children began to organize and press for reform and for compensation. In short order, a class-action lawsuit was brought against the drug companies that made the vaccines with thimerosal. In Britain in 1998, Dr. Andrew Wakefield published a study he had done on autistic children. He found that 8 of 15 parents associated the onset of their child's autism with getting thimerosal-laced MMR vaccine. As was becoming apparent from the experiences of parents with autistic children, Wakefield stated that the digestive problems almost universally experienced by autistic children were caused by thimerosal. He then postulated that the digestive problems led to the onset of autism. Wakefield's study has been universally criticized by the medical establishment, which has pointed out that it did not include both vaccinated and unvaccinated children (a necessary comparison) and that the digestive problems occurred after the children were diagnosed as being autistic; therefore, they could not have caused autism.

Despite the official debunking of his research, parents of autistic children rallied around Wakefield's notion that MMR vaccine caused autism. They called all the studies that showed no linkage between thimerosal and autism "government propaganda." One parents' group obtained copies of CDC internal reports and memos that showed that the agency had anticipated the demand to remove the chemical from vaccines but had done nothing. A large number of studies looked into the connection between thimerosal and autism. Some seemed to correlate the onset of developmental problems with MMR injections. Others found no connection. The problem in all these studies—as in so much research involving environmental toxins—is that because there are so many chemicals and conditions that children, and adults, are exposed to in life, it is extremely hard to find a cause-and-effect relationship between one chemical and one disease. So it was with autism. In spite of these uncertainties, another meeting of vaccine experts in 2000 ended with all but one of the doctors in attendance agreeing that there was probably a strong correlation between thimerosal in MMR and autism. Yet as often happened, no sooner had this strong correlation been made than a new study revealed little or no connection between the two. In 2001, two studies came up with conflicting results; one found that it was "biologically plausible" that thimerosal caused autism, the other that the chemical had no negative health effects. The evidence was confusing: People on each side of the issue felt that their belief was stronger, and each criticized the other.

As of 2006, more than 5,000 lawsuits were pending before the U.S. National Vaccine Injury Compensation Program. Another 4,300 cases were waiting in the wings. The researchers at the CDC felt that they were under siege. They were stung by accusations that the work they did, which they intended only for good, was seen as doing so much harm. By this time, thimerosal had been removed from MMR and other vaccines. Experts and researchers have been keeping careful records of the number of cases of autism reported in the years since thimerosal was banned. If the number of autism cases has declined since thimerosal was banned, then it is likely that the chemical had some role in causing the disease. If the number of autism cases has stayed the same, then thimerosal could be "acquitted" of the charge—and something else has to be responsible for the "epidemic" of autism. Some recent studies suggest that there is a genetic basis for autism. However, no one can explain why these genes are popping up more often now than ever before. Other researchers have found evidence that autism begins before the infant is born. If that is true, then autism may be caused by some environmental toxin inadvertently taken into the pregnant mother's body.

The debate about thimerosal-laden vaccines and autism is not over, and will probably not be resolved until the true cause of autism is found. In the meantime, parents are encouraged to have their babies vaccinated with MMR, DTP, and all the other prescribed childhood vaccines. Some parents remain skeptical and continue to refuse to have their children vaccinated. It's a problem and a debate that will likely continue for a long time.

New Challenges, New Frontiers

The controversies—and pending lawsuits—surrounding the supposed negative health effects of vaccines have had a dampening effect on the development of new vaccines. However, there are dedicated medical researchers working hard to find new vaccines, and new types of vaccines, to prevent—and, hopefully, eventually to eliminate—diseases. In some cases, government health agencies are providing funding and other incentives to encourage drug companies in this research.

FROM GENES TO IMMUNITY

Medical science has come a long way since the time when all vaccines were made either with killed pathogens or attenuated germs. Today, advanced research is creating vaccines that contain only a few bits of genetic material from a pathogen. The genetic material being used, a few **nucleotide** sequences from a pathogen's DNA, does not contain the genes responsible for causing the disease. Yet these bits of DNA are sufficient to stimulate an immune response and initiate the production of antibodies against the disease. For this reason, DNA vaccines are considered to be very safe.

DNA vaccines are made using **plasmids**, or tiny **organelles**, taken from harmless bacteria. In some cases, genetic engineers change the DNA in the plasmid until it closely resembles the DNA in a pathogen. In other cases, harmless bits of a germ's DNA are inserted into the plasmid, where it becomes part of the plasmid's genes. In all cases, the altered plasmid is processed to reproduce countless clones of itself. The cloned plasmids are used in the DNA vaccine. When the vaccine is injected, some plasmids move into the nucleus of body cells, where they begin reproducing genes that have the pathogen's DNA. This triggers an immune response in the body, and antibodies are created against the germ that causes the disease.

Traditional vaccines are injected into a muscle, but some newer DNA vaccines can be given in a less painful way. Some DNA vaccines have been designed to be effective when they are given as a nasal spray. Researchers are also testing vaccines made by bombarding gold particles with bits of germ DNA. A DNA-coated gold patch is then placed on top of the skin. The germ DNA moves under the skin and into cells, where it triggers an immune response.

DNA vaccines are currently being developed to fight several serious diseases, including Ebola, dengue fever, and West Nile virus. A type of DNA vaccine is also being tested to prevent Alzheimer's disease, which causes memory loss in older adults. This vaccine seems to stop the accumulation of harmful substances in the brain of a person with Alzheimer's.

The key to an effective vaccine is finding out which bits of the germ generate a strong immune response without actually making a person sick. Sometimes the most effective bits are not part of the germ at all. Recently, researchers in Ireland discovered a harmless component of the *Staphylococcus* (*Staph*) bacterium that initiates an immune response in the body. (*Staph* germs cause a wide variety of infections, some of them potentially life threatening.) The scientists knew that *Staph* bacteria grow in colonies consisting of many cells. These colonies create a kind of coating, or biofilm, in the body. In studying the biofilm, the researchers found that the "glue" that holds the cells together can be used to make a safe and effective vaccine. The glue does not cause disease, but it is an antigen. When fully developed, this may be the first ever "sticky glue" vaccine.

How Plasmid Vaccines are Made

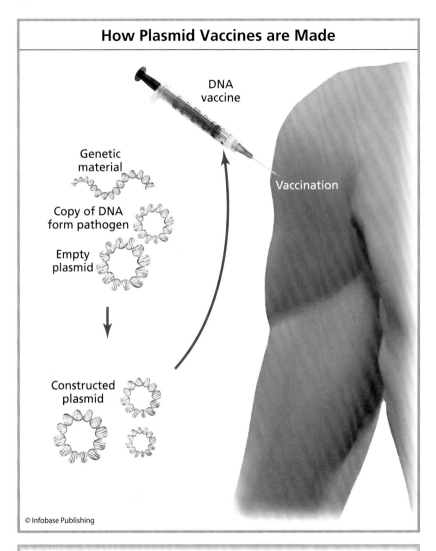

DNA vaccine

Genetic material

Copy of DNA form pathogen

Empty plasmid

Constructed plasmid

Vaccination

© Infobase Publishing

Figure 8.1 This diagram shows how plasmid vaccines are made. Some of a plasmid's DNA is snipped off by a chemical called a restriction enzyme. Then a bit of the pathogen's DNA is removed. It is inserted into the gap in the plasmid's DNA. The plasmid is then put back into a bacterium, which begins reproducing many copies, or clones, of itself. Each clone has a bit of the pathogen DNA. When the plasmid vaccine is injected into a person, the pathogen DNA generates an immune response and the formation of antibodies.

Researchers are also working on vaccines that contain synthetic, or human-made, antigens. Subunit and cell wall vaccines that are taken directly from the pathogen are already in use. Now, however, scientists are attempting to make imitation germ parts for use in vaccines. In their labs, scientists are creating synthetic germ cell walls (out of types of sugar called *polysaccharides*) and bits of imitation antigen protein, or **peptides**. The synthetic components in the vaccine cannot cause disease because they have never been part of a germ. Yet because they are exact copies of parts of the germ, they initiate antibody production. A synthetic peptide vaccine is being tested to fight malaria, and so far the vaccine looks promising.

One new variation of the subunit vaccine is called a vehicle vaccine. This new vaccine uses only a "messenger" gene from the germ. This messenger gene produces chemicals that alert the immune system to the germ's presence. A vehicle vaccine contains a germ messenger gene that is placed inside a harmless bacterium, which is the vehicle. Once inside the body, the messenger gene stimulates an immune response and the production of antibodies. Scientists are still trying to figure out what the best vehicle is for each germ. Researchers have found that a certain strain of bacteria is a good vehicle for a new tuberculosis vaccine. Similar bacteria are being tested to carry the messenger genes from pathogens that cause tetanus, Lyme disease, and even malaria.

Malaria is a disease caused by a parasite, and it has proven very difficult to fight. Scientists in Colombia, South America, have created a synthetic vaccine against malaria that is made with lab-created chemicals, some of which mimic key malaria proteins. The synthetic proteins in the vaccine were chosen because they control important parts of the complicated infection process inside the body. Because the vaccine contains no pathogen at all, it is proving to be very safe. This vaccine is still being tested.

VACCINES AGAINST CANCER

In the 1970s, Dr. William Coley was treating patients and doing research at New York's Sloane Kettering Memorial Hospital, which specializes in cancer treatment. During the course of his practice, Dr. Coley noticed that when some cancer patients got an infection, their tumors would shrink. Dr. Coley concluded, correctly, that the

Eating Vaccines

One of the newest—and most controversial—areas of vaccine research involves inserting bits of pathogen DNA into food plants. The germ DNA is added to the plant seed, so every cell in the plant, such as a tomato, contains it. When a person buys and eats the tomato, he or she eats the bits of germ DNA, which trigger an immune response and the generation of antibodies against the disease caused by the germ. Some of the plants currently being implanted with germ DNA include tomatoes, corn, potatoes, bananas, lettuce, rice, and soybeans. Drug companies envision fields of vaccine-producing crops all over the world. In one meal, a person could be inoculated against a whole host of serious diseases. Injecting people with vaccines for each disease would no longer be necessary.

Many people think this avenue of research should be abandoned because it is too risky. They point out that plants exchange genes with each other all the time. Thus, it would not take long for all or most plants to contain pathogenic DNA. What effect would this have on the insects, birds, deer, and all the other animals that feed on these plants? Might insects and wildlife be harmed by eating plants containing a DNA vaccine intended for humans? Critics point out that once these genes are out in the environment, they are impossible to control. Implanting pathogenic DNA in plants might have serious implications for humans, as well. For example, what might be the consequences of eating vaccines every time you eat food over the course of your whole life? How much vaccine is too much? And what about people who may be allergic to a particular vaccine? How could they avoid it if it is found in nearly all food plants? This type of research is ongoing, but it raises many troubling questions.

infection activated the patients' immune system. The stronger immune system not only fought off the infection but also battled the cancer. His research confirmed that the boosted immune response actually killed cancer cells and reduced the size of tumors. Dr. Coley spent the rest of his life looking for vaccines that could initiate an immune response that would kill cancer cells. Dr. Coley did develop a killed bacteria vaccine that shrank tumors, but the effects of the vaccine did not last, and the cancer always grew back.

Today, researchers recognize that Dr. Coley's vaccine did not work very well because it was non-specific. That is, it did not target the specific germs or proteins associated with different types of cancer. Though the vast majority of cancers are not caused by viruses, scientists are finding that viruses or other pathogens, as well as specific proteins, sometimes play a role in the growth and/or spread of cancer in the body.

One group of researchers has found that a type of herpes virus seems to be associated with one kind of brain tumor. Their research shows that the virus seems to help the tumor grow and spread. The investigators developed a vaccine to generate an immune response against this virus. Initial trials show that the vaccine delays re-growth of the tumor and prolongs overall survival among patients. Another research team discovered that a type of brain tumor had a particular protein on the surface of the cancer cells. They developed a vaccine that targets this protein. The vaccine has been shown to stimulate a strong immune response against the cancer cells.

A different team of researchers has discovered a vaccine that may prevent or treat women who have a gene called HER-2. This gene often causes a very aggressive form of breast cancer that is difficult to treat. The researchers created a vaccine that contains two important components. One component is DNA that codes for the development of HER-2 receptors on breast tissue cells. The second component is a chemical that stimulates the immune system. Both components are inserted into bacterial plasmids, which are injected into the body. Laboratory tests show that the vaccine stimulates a strong immune response, including killer T cells and antibodies against the HER-2 receptors. The killer T cells attack and kill the cells with the cancer-inducing HER-2 receptors, and the antibodies remain in the body to kill any new cancer cells that may develop. Lab studies have shown that this vaccine provides complete protection against HER-2 breast cancer. Clinical trials of this promising vaccine are ongoing.

This new breast cancer vaccine resembles many other cancer vaccines that are being developed in that it stimulates the immune system to attack and kill cancer cells that have unique receptors on their surface. Remember, the immune system is designed not to kill the body's own "self" cells. Cancer cells are, in most ways, "self" cells because they are body cells that grow out of control. It was the discovery that cancer cells have unique surface receptors that has led researchers to begin developing vaccines that stimulate an immune response against these harmful "self" cells. Scientists are currently developing vaccines to fight lymphoma (a cancer of lymph cells) and cancer of the intestines. A totally successful vaccine that produces antibodies against cancer is still not a reality, but researchers are coming closer to realizing that goal every day as they learn more about cancer cells, antibodies, and vaccines.

THE ELUSIVE FLU

Nearly every winter, some type of influenza A—the flu—sweeps through populations around the world. The very young and the very old are advised to get a flu shot, a vaccine to help prevent or to limit the seriousness of the flu, should they get it. Influenza A has been around for centuries, yet a vaccine remains elusive. Why is developing a flu vaccine so difficult?

Influenza A is caused by a virus. This particular virus **mutates**, or changes its genetic makeup, very quickly. In fact, the flu virus has a different genetic makeup almost every year. This means that last year's flu vaccine will not be very effective against this year's flu virus. In most years, the flu virus's genes change a little bit. This is called genetic drift, in which just a few genes mutate. After a year of genetic drift, last year's flu vaccine may limit the seriousness of a flu infection. Every decade or so, however, the influenza A virus undergoes a more dramatic change in its genes; this change is called a genetic shift. No one knows why this great change occurs. After a genetic shift, no previous vaccine is able to combat the altered flu virus. When a genetic shift occurs, widespread outbreaks of flu may sweep across the world, infecting and killing many people. The antibodies people may have from previous bouts of flu are useless in fighting the new genetic strain of influenza.

Figure 8.2   This micrograph shows cancer cells growing and dividing. The surface of cancer cells contains proteins and receptors that are absent on normal body cells.

As of 2008, public health officials around the world are keeping a keen eye on the "bird flu," a new strain of influenza A that has struck and killed people in Asia. Like other strains of influenza A, bird flu originates in non-human animals—in this case, birds and other fowl, such as chickens. All cases of bird flu in Asia have occurred among people who kept fowl around their home for food. So far, scientists believe that people can get bird flu only from infected birds. However, they worry that the influenza A virus may mutate to enable it to be transmitted from an infected person to other people. If the virus mutates to permit human-to-human transmission, another flu

pandemic may occur. Governments are funding research into developing a vaccine against bird flu. The problem is that when the virus mutates to become transmissible from person to person, its genes will be very different from those it has today. Thus, any vaccine developed now may not be effective against the newly mutated virus. Still, health officials are hoping that a vaccine against the current form of bird flu will be of some help in limiting the severity of a flu pandemic, should it occur. Similar research is ongoing to prevent a pandemic of the "swine flu" that occurred in many parts of the world in 2009 to 2010.

In 2008, British researchers announced that they had developed what they called a "universal flu vaccine." This new vaccine does not target those parts of the virus that tend to mutate year after year. The parts of the flu virus that mutate most rapidly are proteins on the surface of the virus. Thus, the British investigators concentrated on making a vaccine using proteins from inside the virus. These internal

The 1918 Flu Pandemic

A pandemic is a worldwide epidemic of a disease. In 1918, a new and lethal strain of influenza A worked its deadly way around the world. The genetic shift that had occurred in the flu virus during the winter of 1918 made it one of the most deadly flu viruses ever. Tens of millions of people were stricken with the flu, and millions died. The virulent disease killed most of its victims within two days. Others who died had contracted the flu about two weeks after first getting the disease. Many of these people did not die of the flu itself but from other illnesses, such as pneumonia, that overwhelmed their weakened immune systems. Scientists today suggest that the violence of the immune response might have caused many of the quick deaths from the 1918 flu. The majority of those who died were young people and teenagers who had robust immune systems. Their immune response was so strong that it may have overwhelmed their bodies.

proteins do not change nearly as much as the ones on the outside. Trials of this universal flu vaccine are underway. If it is shown to protect people against the flu virus for several years, it may turn out to be the single successful vaccine scientists have been seeking for so long.

BIOTERRORISM AND OTHER CHALLENGES

The world has been free of smallpox for years. There are now vaccines to prevent all kinds of terrible and deadly infectious diseases. Can scientists proclaim victory over disease and stop doing research on new vaccines? Hardly.

Many public health and national security officials worry about the threat of bioterrorism—of deadly disease germs getting into the hands of terrorists who release the germs to kill large numbers of people. Smallpox has been eradicated; yet there is the tiny possibility that terrorists may get some smallpox viruses, alter their genes a bit, and release them in a large city where smallpox would spread rapidly and kill many. The threat of bioterrorism was one of the reasons the United States and Russia decided to retain their stockpiles of smallpox viruses. They believed that these viruses could be used to develop a vaccine if terrorists somehow obtained smallpox germs and used them against a population. Experts consider smallpox and anthrax to be the two pathogens most likely to be used in a bioterrorism attack.

Bioterrorism poses many challenges to researchers and health officials. Researchers must have tools and techniques for quickly analyzing a mutated pathogen and developing a vaccine to prevent the disease it causes. Drug companies must also be prepared to produce many millions of doses of the vaccine very quickly, and public health officials throughout a nation must be ready to vaccinate millions of people in a short period of time. Just in case there is a delay in vaccination, a country should also stockpile a huge supply of antibiotics to treat people who get anthrax or other bacterial diseases.

All in all, there are many reasons to continue the search for newer and better vaccines. Some diseases, such as malaria, still kill millions every year. We need vaccines to prevent these diseases. Other diseases, like influenza A and tuberculosis, mutate rapidly or become resistant to currently available treatments. We need ongoing vaccine research to combat these diseases, too. Cancer may one day be prevented or cured with vaccines. As long as bioterrorism is a threat, we cannot let our guard down; we must continue to develop vaccines that are quick and easy to produce. The more scientists learn about cells, the immune system, and disease, the more vaccines they will likely develop to prevent, cure, or treat diseases, such as Alzheimer's, that once were thought to be beyond the reach of vaccines.

Glossary

acquired immune system   The part of the immune system that is activated by the innate immune system and generates powerful disease-fighting cells, such as killer T cells

antibody   Proteins produced by B cells that match and bind to specific pathogens that invade the body; antibodies may remain in the body a long time and confer immunity to a specific disease.

antigen   Any part of a pathogen, or disease-causing agent, that initiates an immune system response in the body

antitoxin   A substance, like a vaccine, that is used to initiate an immune response against the toxins produced by disease-causing agents

artificial vaccine   A human-made vaccine that contains no pathogen or pathogen parts; it is constructed of proteins and amino acids identical to those on the surface of a particular pathogen in order to mimic the pathogen.

attenuate   To weaken, as a vaccine, via dilution, heat, radiation, or other method; an attenuated vaccine is made from disease agents that are so weakened that they don't cause disease.

autism   A behavioral, neurological disease that afflicts young children; the afflicted children have difficulty relating to people or to the outside world.

bacilli (singular, bacillus)   A type of single-celled organism; a type of bacteria that often produces spores.

bacteria (singular, bacterium)   A type of single-celled organism (a prokaryote that has free-floating DNA); bacteria are everywhere, but only a few cause disease.

B cells   The cells of the acquired immune system that create antibodies

chicken pox   A viral disease that causes body sores; it may be serious or even deadly.

clone   A genetically identical copy of a living thing

contagious   Characteristic of a disease that can be passed from one person to another

DNA   A tiny unit of genetic material consisting of one or more pairs of substances called nucleotides. DNA controls the inheritance of traits.

DTP   A vaccine given to prevent diphtheria, tetanus, and pertussis (whooping cough)

endemic   Native to a specific place

epidemic   An outbreak of disease over a large region and affecting many people

formalin   A solution that includes formaldehyde, which is used as a preservative

gene   A unit of inheritance; it is a group of proteins (nucleotides) that code for a trait or body function

germ theory   The theory that one particular disease-causing agent causes only one specific disease

hemorrhagic   Causing bleeding, as in some diseases that cause internal bleeding

immune   Resistant to a disease because of antibodies in the body that fight the illness

immune memory   Refers to the antibodies that remain active in the body to fight reinfection by a pathogen

immune system   The body system whose cells combat any invaders, including disease-causing agents, that enter the body

innate immune system   The non-specific part of the immune system; the cells of the innate immune system are the first to attack invaders in the body.

inoculation   Injection or introduction into the body of any substance that will fight or prevent disease by generating an immune response

larva (plural, larvae)   The immature, juvenile form of some organisms

lymphatic system   A body-wide circulatory system involved in transporting proteins, removing cell debris, and serving as a conduit for immune system cells, such as lymphocytes, which reside in and/ or are created in lymph nodes in various parts of the body

lymphocytes   The cells of the acquired immune system, such as T cells and B cells

macrophage   A "big eater" cell that is part of the innate immune system and is one of the first immune system cells to start attacking and killing invaders and pathogens

measles   A highly contagious viral disease that causes a rash and may cause blindness

meningitis   A viral disease that causes an inflammation of the membrane that surrounds the brain and the spinal cord

microbe   A general term referring to any microscopic organism (or virus)

microscope   Equipment used to enlarge or magnify an object, usually one that cannot be seen by the unaided eye; light microscopes use glass lenses and can magnify objects up to 2,000 times. Electron microscopes use beams of electrons and electromagnetism to magnify objects up to 2 million times.

MMPV   A vaccine given to prevent measles, mumps, rubella, and varicella-zoster (which causes chicken pox)

MMR   A vaccine given to prevent measles, mumps, and rubella

motor neuron   A nerve cell that controls body movement (muscles)

mumps   A childhood disease caused by a virus that causes swelling of the salivary glands

mutate   To change an organism's or virus's genes; a mutation is a change in an organism's or virus's genes.

natural killer cells Cells of the innate immune system that are called in by macrophages to help destroy invaders in the body

neuron A cell that is part of the nervous system

nucleotide One of four proteins that make up DNA

organelle A small structure within a cell that carries out specific cell functions; for example, the cell nucleus or chloroplasts in a plant cell

pandemic A worldwide epidemic

parasite Any agent or organism that lives off another organism in such a way that the "host" organism is harmed, while only the parasite benefits

pathogen Any disease-causing agent (such as bacteria or viruses)

peptide A protein

pertussis A bacterial disease that causes convulsive coughing (whooping cough)

phagocyte Immune system cells, such as macrophages, that "eat" and destroy body invaders

placebo A deliberately ineffective substance, such as a sugar pill, given during drug trials to contrast its effects with those of the active drug

plasmid A ring of bacterial DNA that easily and quickly reproduces

polio A disease caused by a virus that, in its most severe form, can cause paralysis

protein A three-dimensional, folded structure made up of amino acids that does not change its shape when it comes in contact with cells or other proteins

pus A collection of white blood cells at the site of an infection

quarantine To separate the ill from the well; to keep the sick away from the healthy

receptor A protein formation on the surface of a cell; it is designed to bind to a nutrient or another substance (such as an antibody) that has the same configuration of proteins.

recombinant vaccine   A vaccine that is made with only the pathogen envelope; the inner, disease-causing parts of the pathogen are removed, leaving only the harmless envelope.

rubella   A relatively mild viral disease, with symptoms similar to measles; it is also called German measles.

serum   The clear, fluid part of blood that remains after other parts, such as clotting factors, are removed

smallpox   An often deadly viral disease that many times causes epidemics; it is now virtually eradicated.

spontaneous generation   The outdated, disproven idea that life could arise spontaneously from matter such as rotting meat

spore   A primitive type of reproductive body, usually covered in a protective coating, produced mainly by fungi and some microbes

subunit vaccine   A vaccine made from tiny bits of a pathogen

T cell   A powerful lymphocyte, differentiated in the thymus, that is antigen specific and kills pathogens; there are several types of T cells in the acquired immune system.

thimerosal   A preservative formerly widely used in vaccines to prevent contamination by bacteria; as a mercury compound, it has been linked by some to neurological damage, particularly autism, in young children who got vaccines containing it.

toxin   In medicine, a poison given off by a pathogen

vaccination   An injection or introduction into the body of a vaccine to prevent a disease

vaccine   A preparation of a disease-causing agent that is introduced into the body to generate the production of antibodies against that particular disease

varicella-zoster   The virus that causes chicken pox

viral chimera   A vaccine against a viral disease that is made with only a few bits of virus DNA

virus   A strange, not-living, not-dead type of matter that is much smaller than bacteria and consists only of proteins and genetic material; some viruses cause disease, but many others do not.

Bibliography

Allen, Arthur. *Vaccine: The Controversial Story of Medicine's Greatest Lifesaver*. New York: W.W. Norton & Company, 2007.

Ballard, Carol. *From Cowpox to Antibiotics: Discovering Vaccines and Medicines*. Chicago: Heinemann Library, 2006.

Burge, Michael C. *Vaccines: Preventing Disease*. San Diego: Lucent Books, 1992.

Collier, James Lincoln. *Vaccines*. New York: Benchmark Books, 2004.

Matsumoto, Gary. *Vaccine A: The Covert Government Experiment That's Killing Our Soldiers*. New York: Basic Books, 2004.

Naff, Clay Farris, ed. *Vaccines*. Farmington Hills, Mich.: Greenhaven Press, 2005.

Offit, Paul A. *The Cutter Incident*. New Haven: Yale University Press, 2005.

Peters, Stephanie True. *The Battle Against Polio*. New York: Benchmark Books, 2005.

———. *The 1918 Flu Pandemic*. New York: Benchmark Books, 2005.

Sherrow, Victoria. *Polio Epidemic: Crippling Virus Outbreak*. Berkeley Heights, N.J.: Enslow Publishers, 2001.

Tucker, Jonathan B. *Scourge: The Once and Future Threat of Smallpox*. New York: Atlantic Monthly Press, 2001.

Further Resources

Alpin, Elaine Marie. *Germ Hunter: A Story About Louis Pasteur*. Minneapolis: Lerner Publishing, 2004.

Ballard, Carol. *Body Focus: The Immune System*. Chicago: Heinemann Library, 2004.

Bankston, John. *Jonas Salk and the Polio Vaccine*. Bear, Del.: Mitchell Lane Publishers, 2001.

Bloom, Barry. *The Vaccine Book*. Boston: Academic Press, 2002.

Bookchin, Debbie and Jim Schumacher. *The Virus and the Vaccine*. New York: St. Martin's Press, 2004.

Donnellan, William L. *The Miracle of Immunity*. New York: Benchmark Books, 2003.

Friedlander, Mark P. and Terry M. Phillips. *The Immune System*. Minneapolis: Lerner Publications, 1998.

Naden, Corrine J. and Rose Blue. *Jonas Salk: Polio Pioneer*. Brookfield, Conn.: Millbrook Press, 2001.

Nardo, Don. *Vaccines*. San Diego: Lucent Books, 2002.

Ridgway, Tom. *Smallpox*. New York: Rosen Publishing, 2001.

Tocci, Salvatore. *Jonas Salk: Creator of the Polio Vaccine*. Berkeley Heights, N.J.: Enslow Publishers, 2003.

Web Sites

Allied Vaccine Group
www.vaccine.org

This vaccine-education organization's site has links to and information from many leading children's health Web sites.

American Academy of Pediatrics
www.aap.org/healthtopics/Immunizations.cfm

This organization represents tens of thousands of pediatricians (children's doctors). The Web site contains information about vaccination and disease.

Centers for Disease Control: Vaccines
www.cdc.gov/vaccines/
> *This U.S. government site contains a wealth of information about all types of vaccines, including research on new vaccines under development.*

World Health Organization: Vaccines
www.who.int/immunization/en/
> *Everything you want to know about global efforts to eradicate disease with vaccines can be found on this Web site.*

How Cancer Vaccines Work
www.howstuffworks.com/cancer-vaccine.htm
> *Here you will find an easy-to-understand explanation of how vaccines help fight cancer.*

Immunization Action Coalition
www.immunize.org/journalarticles/toi_poten.asp
> *This site offers abstracts of journal articles describing research into new vaccines.*

KNOW Vaccines
www.know-vaccines.org/autism.html
> *This site offers information to support the view that vaccines do cause autism.*

Lady Mary Wortley Montagu: Smallpox Vaccination in Turkey
Modern History Sourcebook
www.fordham.edu/halsall/med/montagu-smallpox.html
> *This is a Web site about Lady Montagu's experiences with smallpox vaccination in Turkey.*

National Institute of Allergy and Infectious Diseases
www3.niaid.nih.gov/topics/vaccines/default.htm
> *This is a Web site with comprehensive information about vaccines and their relationship to allergies.*

National Network of Immunization Information
www.immunizationinfo.org
> *This site has a wealth of information on vaccines and immunization. It is an affiliation between of the Infectious Diseases Society of America, the Pediatric Infectious Diseases Society, the American Academy of Pediatrics, the American Nurses Association, the American Academy of Family Physicians, the National Association of Pediatric Nurse Practitioners, the American College of Obstetricians and Gynecolo-*

gists, the University of Texas Medical Branch, the Society for Adoles-cent Medicine, and the American Medical Association.

National Vaccine Information Center

www.909shot.com

This Web site opposes mandatory vaccination of children.

Vaccines and Autism: Autism Information Center (CDC)

www.cdc.gov/vaccinesafety/

This government Web site explains why vaccines do not cause autism.

Vaccination Information

www.vaccineinformation.org

This site contains a great deal of information about vaccines, their ef-fects and side effects, and other useful facts.

The Vaccine Page

www.vaccines.org

This Web site filters up-to-the-minute news about vaccines.

Picture Credits

Index

About the Author

Natalie Goldstein has been a science writer for more than 20 years. She has master's degrees in education from the City College of New York and environmental science from the SUNY College of Environmental Science and Forestry, and has written several science books for children and young adults. She has also written extensively on science and health for elementary school, middle school, and high school textbooks.